CRITICAL GUIDES TO SPANISH TEXTS

3

Valle-Inclán: Tirano Banderas

CRITICAL GUIDES TO SPANISH TEXTS

Edited by

J. E. Varey and A. D. Deyermond

VALLE-INCLÁN

TIRANO BANDERAS

*

VERITY SMITH

Lecturer in Spanish, Westfield College,
University of London

Grant & Cutler Ltd

in association with

Tamesis Books Ltd

1971

© Grant & Cutler Ltd
1971
SBN 900411 24 4

Depósito Legal: M.-16630 - 1971

Printed in Spain by Talleres Gráficos de Ediciones Castilla, S.A.
Maestro Alonso, 23 - Madrid

for

GRANT & CUTLER LTD,
11, BUCKINGHAM STREET, LONDON, W.C.2.

Contents

To Tracy and Francesca

for their cooperation.

Preface

Among Valle-Inclán's novels, *Tirano Banderas* is usually acknow-
ledged to be his masterpiece. It ranks, with the novels of the *Ruedo
ibérico* cycle, as one of the most complex and most demanding of
the reader's attention. In it there is a successful fusion of artistic
elements and subject-matter. The author describes the exploitation
of a banana republic by foreign investors, the callous treatment of
the Amerindian and the struggle of a group of revolutionaries,
availing himself of sophisticated techniques which successfully remove
the novel from the sphere of political pamphleteering. It is impossible
to grasp all the subtleties of *Tirano Banderas* at one reading, but it
repays close scrutiny because in this way one is able to appreciate the
finer points, be they stylistic, thematic or related to one of Valle's
personal preoccupations such as man's understanding of time.

It is my hope that the short analysis of the novel provided in the
following pages will help towards an understanding of Valle's aims
and the subtle, indirect ways used to express them. In writing it I
have relied at times very heavily on Emma Susana Speratti Piñero's
La elaboración artística en Tirano Banderas, a work of fundamental
importance on this novel.

All quotations from the works of Valle-Inclán refer to the *Obras
completas* published by Editorial Plenitud (2 vols, Madrid, 1954), to
which page references are given; *Tirano Banderas* is in vol. II. The
titles of three periodicals have been abbreviated throughout:—
Bulletin of Hispanic Studies: *BHS*; *Nueva Revista de Filología
Hispánica*: *NRFH*; *Revista Hispánica Moderna*: *RHM*.

I

The Plot

From the very beginning of his career as a writer, Valle-Inclán showed indifference to plot as a basic constituent of the novel. For example, in the *Sonatas,* written at a time when he was adhering to the *modernista* credo, Valle seeks to create a mood, an appeal to the senses rather than to the intellect. The same is true of his mature work of the nineteen-twenties, save that aesthetic values are replaced by an analysis of Spanish society and its shortcomings.

Evidently, in *Tirano Banderas* Valle is not directly concerned with Spain but with a former —though imaginary— Spanish possession in the New World, posited therefore on Spanish social and cultural values. However, the character of the country does not mirror accurately that of metropolitan Spain, owing to the presence of the Amerindian, and to differences of climate, environment and language.

The political situation in Tierra Caliente resembles that in many other Latin-American states during periods of dictatorship. The country is a typical 'banana republic' in which foreign powers including the United States, Britain and Germany have a stranglehold on the nation's resources. The head of state is a cruel, repressive and mentally unstable tyrant who, like the country he dominates, is intended as an archetype. The author based his portrayal of Santos Banderas on a number of tyrants such as Argentina's Manuel de Rosas (1835-52), Ecuador's Gabriel García Moreno (1860-75) and Mexico's Porfirio Díaz (1876-1911).

The plot of *Tirano Banderas* can be summarised very briefly. At the outset two facts are established. One of them is that the Tyrant has just suppressed an uprising at a town called Zamalpoa; the second is that a further attempt to oust the dictator is about to be made.

The leader of the new, projected rebellion is a creole of an admirable and unselfish nature called Filomeno Cuevas. He is joined by Domiciano de la Gándara, a former henchman of the Tyrant who has fallen into disgrace. In the prologue Filomeno Cuevas is perfecting his plans to seize the capital of the country, Santa Fe de Tierra Firme. The townspeople are celebrating the Catholic festivals of All Saints and All Souls, so that one kind of disorder is imposed on another: the return to chaos implicit in the communal feast or holiday and the disorder of political violence. In both cases death is in the foreground, since the festivals commemorate the dead, and the projected coup, tragically, will add to their number.

Valle-Inclán then proceeds to give us a detailed picture of the various strata of the community. He considers the Tyrant and his sycophantic followers, a variety of foreign diplomats concerned with petty intrigue and vested interests, the fate of political prisoners in the fortress prison of Santa Mónica, prostitutes, charlatans, rebels, natives, Spanish residents —the whole gamut of Tierra Caliente's society is explored.

At the novel's end the rebels are successful. Tirano Banderas kills his daughter so that she will not fall into the hands of his enemies. He is then shot, and when his corpse has been quartered it is exhibited in the four principal towns of Tierra Caliente. The account of the Tyrant's end is compressed into a single laconic paragraph, free of any comment whatsoever from the author. The apparent objectivity with which Valle views the characters and situations he creates is a feature of nearly all his mature work, a feature, one might add, which he shares with another Spanish writer of the same period, Gabriel Miró. In both cases apparent objectivity makes for sophistication and subtlety in the presentation of a point of view. The writers always have a definite attitude, but it is veiled so that the reader is not wearied by sermons from an omniscient author. He is required instead to consult the images applied by these authors to their characters, for it is these which provide an accurate index of the authors' feelings towards them.

I have said that plot is an unimportant aspect of *Tirano Banderas*. The same holds good for character portrayal, since Valle-Inclán never interested himself in psychological studies. What then are the author's chief aims and preoccupations in this novel? The answer is that, as in the *Ruedo ibérico* novels written at the same period, Valle-Inclán was concerned with an analysis and satire of society. In *Tirano Banderas* Valle studies a typical Latin-American country haunted by a savage dictator. Tierra Caliente is a banana republic dominated by the foreign investor or 'neo-imperialist', a country in which the status of the Amerindian is that of a serf. It is perhaps a sad commentary on human affairs that the political and social organization described by Valle-Inclán in 1926 has altered but little in this area of the world in the forty-five years which have elapsed since the novel's publication.

II

Structure and Time

> Ahora, en algo que estoy escribiendo,
> esta idea de llenar el tiempo como lle-
> naba El Greco el espacio, totalmente
> me preocupa.

Before much attention was paid to Valle-Inclán's later novels, it was customary for critics to dismiss them as obscure and disjointed. It is true that at first glance *Tirano Banderas* appears a bewildering and fragmentary work. For example, the novel is divided into seven parts or main sections. Each one of these is subdivided into a specific number of 'books'. Every 'book' contains a number of short episodes or sequences, some of which, like stage directions, consist of only a few lines.

Tirano Banderas, like the other novels Valle wrote in his maturity, has a very marked dramatic bias, and these brief, tersely written passages are better described as scenes than as chapters. All the scenes in one particular part or section concern one block of characters. The start of a new section indicates that the reader's attention is being transferred to some other part of the town of Santa Fe and to another group of characters.

In addition, the events described in the novel are not narrated in strict chronological order. Those that take place in the prologue seem to bear no relation to those described in the first and subsequent chapters. As in the case of a detective story, the reader has to wait until the very last pages before he is in a position to grasp the meaning of the prologue and make sense of the novel as a whole. Even then, the reader's understanding will be imperfect if he is not aware of Valle-Inclán's interest in number symbolism or his particular understanding of time.

The apparently fragmentary nature of *Tirano Banderas* conceals a structure so symmetrical and sophisticated as to verge on the precious.

a) *Number Symbolism*

Valle-Inclán's marked interest in the occult and in esoteric doctrines emerges in *Tirano Banderas* in two different ways: directly, through the philosophy of the idealistic politician Roque Cepeda, and indirectly, through the very contrived structure imposed on the novel. This is based entirely on two numbers, 3 and 7, which are of great importance in myth, folklore, magic and religion.

A close examination of the novel's structure reveals that each of the seven parts or sections (*partes* in Spanish) is subdivided into a number of 'books'. The pattern that emerges is as follows:

Prologue
Part   I : 3 books
Part   II : 3 books
Part III : 3 books
Part IV : 7 books
Part   V : 3 books
Part VI : 3 books
Part VII : 3 books
Epilogue

Such a structure, in which the central section (7 books) is like the centre of a circle and informs the whole novel with meaning, is by no means unusual in Valle's production. Indeed, *Flor de santidad* (1904), written under the aegis of *Modernismo*, has a similar structure.[1] In addition, Valle had sought to make *Gerifaltes de antaño* (1908), a novel of the *Carlist War* trilogy, equally symmetrical.[2] Other works

---

[1]*Flor de santidad* is divided into 5 sections or *estancias*. Four of these *estancias* are subdivided into 5 chapters while the remaining one, at the novel's centre, contains 6.

[2]There is an unpublished letter by Valle-Inclán addressed to an imaginary critic whom he styles Señor Fantasio, in which he dwells on the organisation of this novel. Valle makes the point that according to his original plan deliberate parallels were established between different chapters. For example, if the novel consisted of, say, 30 chapters, those characters who figured prominently in chapter 1 would also be to the forefront in chapter 30. Similarly, those described in chapter 2 would re-appear in 29, etc. . . In the final version —for

with a symmetrical structure of this kind are *La lámpara maravillosa, Divinas palabras,* the first edition of *Luces de bohemia,* and the two completed novels of the *Ruedo ibérico* cycle, *La corte de los milagros* and *Viva mi dueño.* The most interesting and complex examples are, without doubt, those provided by the *Ruedo ibérico* novels.

It remains to determine why in *Tirano Banderas* Valle-Inclán should have employed 3 and 7, since these numbers do not figure prominently in the structure of other works he wrote. Evidently there exist a variety of numerological systems from which Valle-Inclán could have made his choice. However, granted his keen interest in the Gnostic heresy —something which is borne out in many passages of *La lámpara maravillosa*— it is likely that he opted for their number symbolism.

According to the Gnostics, matter was evil and fate had seven demonic agents. The world of phenomena emanated from the triadic harmony of Being, Life and Intellect.[3] Thus the association of 7 with evil and of 3 with good could well represent the confrontation of the two conflicting forces in the novel: tyranny incarnate in Santos Banderas, and liberty in the characters of Filomeno Cuevas and Roque Cepeda.[4] If this hypothesis is accepted, then the fact that the central section (IV) contains 7 books implies that Valle took a very pessimistic view of the revolution's prospects. A similarly grim outlook is to be found in the completed novels of the *Ruedo ibérico* in which the contents of the central books concern chaos and death.

b) *Time*

Without doubt, time must be placed among Valle's chief pre-

rather trivial reasons— the original symmetry was marred. But the idea remained in Valle's mind and he perfected it years later in *La corte de los milagros* and *Viva mi dueño.*

[3]Christopher Butler, *Number Symbolism* (London, 1970), 36.

[4]It is worth noting that when Roque Cepeda is incarcerated in Santa Mónica, he occupies cell number 3 (*T.B.,* 792).

occupations, forming one of the most engrossing facets of his work. As in the case of number symbolism, Valle's fascination with time can be traced back to his *modernista* phase.[5] One should also bear in mind that it is a subject whose complexities have been given much attention by writers of this century in particular, and Valle-Inclán was always very sensitive to artistic and philosophic currents in Western Europe.

The time-span of *Tirano Banderas*, as is also the case with *La corte de los milagros* (1927),[6] is exceedingly short. The novel covers a period of three days, and most of the events take place on the religious festivals of All Saints and All Souls. Since the imaginary state of Tierra Caliente is based on Mexico, the choice of these two days is not fortuitous. The days Valle has chosen underline the novel's principal theme, which is death.

As I have already mentioned, the events are not narrated in strict, chronological fashion. For example, the incidents described in the prologue take place before those related in the bulk of the novel, and time only begins to move forward again near the very end of the narrative when the rebels attack the town of Santa Fe. It becomes obvious as one reads *Tirano Banderas* that some of the events are to be understood as occurring simultaneously. Valle, who was interested in the Gnostics, accepted their view of time, whereby the Christian linear conception of time (unfolding in a straight line from the

---

[5]The chronology of the four *Sonatas* proves, on examination, not to make sense. For example, in *Otoño* Bradomín is already an ageing man whilst his mistress Concha is but thirty-one. Yet at one point Bradomín speaks of having played with her as a child in the gardens of the Pazo de Brandeso (*O.C.*, II, 140). This could be an oversight on Valle's part, but granted his preoccupation with time, it is more likely that even at this comparatively early stage he is showing scorn for "los caminos del tiempo, que son los caminos del mundo" (II, 780).

[6]In the case of *La corte de los milagros* −a considerably longer novel than *Tirano Banderas*− the period covered is of 9 days: from Easter Sunday (which fell on April 12 in 1868) to the death of the Prime Minister, Narváez, on April 21. See G. Díaz-Plaja, *Las estéticas de Valle-Inclán* (Madrid, 1965), 253.

Creation to the day of Judgment) is replaced by a cyclical interpretation. In addition, like the Gnostics, Valle believed that it was
only the lower terrestrial world which was condemned to endure
time, while the upper world was timeless. So for Valle-Inclán eternity
could be equated with the instant of time in which everything in the
universe, past, present and to come, is revealed to man. He dwells on
this point in the "breve noticia" at the beginning of *La media noche*
(1917), an account of a visit to the Western Front during the
Great War. Here Valle deplores the fact that the writer is hampered
by having to describe events in chronological order, something
which falsifies his material: "Acontece que, al escribir de la guerra, el
narrador que antes fue testigo da a los sucesos un enlace cronológico
puramente accidental, nacido de la humana y geométrica limitación
que nos veda ser a la vez en varias partes" (631). He then adds that
if the author were able to be in various places at one and the same
time, his vision of the war would be radically different: ". . . de cierto
tendría de la guerra una visión, una emoción y una concepción en
todo distinta de la que puede tener el mísero testigo, sujeto a las
leyes geométricas de la materia corporal y mortal" (631). Valle
concludes by saying that he is conscious of a sense of failure:

> Yo, torpe y vano de mí, quise ser centro y tener de la guerra una
> vision astral, fuera de geometría y de cronología, como si el alma,
> descarnada ya, mirase a la tierra desde su estrella. He fracasado
> en el empeño, mi droga índica en esta ocasión me negó su efluvio
> maravilloso (632).

In *Tirano Banderas* Valle seeks to make good his earlier failure by
describing events occurring simultaneously in different parts of the
town of Santa Fe and its environs. So the novel resembles a Cubist
painting in that various elements are abruptly juxtaposed: links and
connecting threads between one episode and the next are conspicuous
by their absence. Antonio Risco has noted how Valle's desire to
exploit the possibilities of the present to its maximum tends to blur
the reader's consciousness of the passage of time:

Descompone la acción en un sinfín de hechos que llegan a reba-
sarla y a ahogarla. Toma pequeñas unidades de tiempo y las rellena
de menudos acontecimientos que en tan precaria extensión revelan
todo un mundo como la gota de agua observada al microsopio. El
lector se extravía en tal pluralidad, olvida los puntos de referencia
y llega a perder conciencia de la cronología.[7]

But, as I indicated earlier, this deliberate fragmentation does not
mean that the later novels lack formal unity. This is provided by the
rigid symmetry of the underlying structure and, in the case of *Tirano
Banderas*, by the ominous figure of the Tyrant himself who dominates
the life of Tierra Caliente and haunts the minds of its citizens.

Abrupt changes of scene —highly reminiscent of film cuts— are
sometimes used in this novel to indicate that two events in different
localities are occurring simultaneously. The last words in part II are
spoken by the Tyrant who is now determined to arrest one of his
henchmen, Domiciano de la Gándara, for a peccadillo he is supposed
to have committed. He says to his Chief of Police: "Al macaneador
de mi compadre, será prudente arrestarlo esta noche, Mayor del
Valle." At once the reader's attention is switched to a brothel in the
town (el Congal de Cucarachita), where Domiciano de la Gándara is
found in the company of one of the prostitutes, Lupita la Romántica.
In the ensuing scenes of this 'book' there are further effects of
simultaneity, reminiscent again of film cuts. When the police enter
the brothel to arrest Domiciano, cuts from the pursuer to the pursued
indicate that their actions are taking place at the same moment of
time.

Valle-Inclán also avails himself of Lupita la Romántica to achieve
an effect of simultaneity. According to a charlatan called Doctor
Polaco, Lupita could become, with his help, an excellent medium.
There is, however, one drawback, this being that Lupita is unable to
foresee the future or reconstruct the past: her psychic powers are

---

[7] Antonio Risco, *La estética de Valle-Inclán* (Madrid, 1966), 140.

limited to the present. Valle, who is extremely sophisticated and
subtle, is making two points in this way. Since it is his purpose that
time should stand still in certain parts of this novel, Lupita is useful
to him because of the very limitations of her powers.[8] Thus, when
in a state of trance she speaks of someone who goes up "una escalera
muy grande" and then "entra por una puerta donde hay un centinela",
the reader is taken back to the end of the previous section when
Tirano Banderas mounts a flight of stairs. So the reader knows that
Lupita's vision actually coincides with the Tyrant's action. But by
picking on a sentimental prostitute whose proposed manager is a
charlatan, and by denying her the gift of prophecy, Valle makes of
Lupita a typical *esperpento* figure. She is part of the "visión degra-
dadora" as Díaz-Plaja has termed it.

One point that remains to be considered is the year in which the
action is set. In *Tirano Banderas*, as in many other of his works,
Valle-Inclán proves elusive on the question of dates and the reader is
obliged to work this out for himself through the odd allusion made
by one or other of the characters. That Valle was well-nigh obsessed
with the period around 1870 is beyond dispute. His preoccupation
with this period is attested by any number of his works, including the
Sonata de invierno, the *Carlist War* trilogy, the *Comedias bárbaras*
and the *Ruedo ibérico* cycle. So it comes as no surprise to discover
that the events narrated in *Tirano Banderas* take place in 1873. This
can be deduced from the musings of one of the Spanish characters
in the novel, Don Celestino Galindo. The Spanish Minister in Tierra
Caliente tries to bribe him by making out that he will obtain an
important government post for Don Celes in the home country. Don
Celes, thrilled to the marrow by this prospect, thinks to himself:

---

[8]In *La lámpara maravillosa* (1916) Valle dwells on the nature of prophetic
vision in terms which are very relevant here: "Acaso el don profético no sea la
visión de lo venidero, sino una más perfecta visión que del momento fugaz de
nuestra vida consigue el alma quebrantando sus lazos con la carne" (II, 568).

"Emilio le llamaría por cable" (799). The Emilio in question has to be Emilio Castelar who was Prime Minister in 1873 at the time of the first ill-fated republican experiment in Spain.

The apparently fragmentary form of *Tirano Banderas*, coupled with its very real stylistic difficulties, is the chief obstacle to the understanding of this novel. Once Valle-Inclán's particular conception of and obsession with time have been grasped, the underlying structure is not only clear but becomes a positive attribute of the work. It is satisfying to be presented with a novel that has a neat, circular structure imposed on it to underline the meaning of the whole. In the words of Ricardo Gullón: "No es casualidad que el prólogo y el epílogo se den la mano; que muerda el uno la cola del otro, pues este comenzar donde se acaba . . . es excelente modo de señalar . . . la esterilidad del movimiento."[9]

[9]"Técnicas de Valle-Inclán," *Papeles de Son Armadans,* XLIII (1966), 35-6.

III

Sources and Genesis

a) Sources

Valle-Inclán might well be described as the source-hunter's dream.[10] He believed, rightly, that pure originality on the author's part was less important than what could be created from an idea, incident or character inspired by the text of another. Early critics of Valle-Inclán's work tended to be censorious on the subject of his so-called plagiarisms, but in more recent years moral indignation has been replaced by a more dispassionate and rational attitude to the subject. In the words of Joseph H. Silverman:

> La literatura era una de sus fuentes de inspiración más ricas y variadas. Fuera de quien fuera, la palabra escrita, tanto como la vida misma, era materia prima de su arte, pábulo indispensable de su numen. La originalidad para Valle-Inclán, para cualquier auténtico artista, no es más que una manera inédita de combinar materiales trillados o exóticos para formar una totalidad nueva.[11]

Conscious of being branded a plagiarist, Valle provided his own defence in conversation with Alfonso Reyes. Valle, Reyes records, felt that a borrowing from another source

> equivale a tomar un rincón del cuadro de las *Meninas*... e incrustarlo en una tela mucho mayor, añadiéndole retazos por todos lados ... Ya, en Anatole France ... Santa Catalina observa, con encantadora pedantería: "La imaginación no crea: combina y compara".[12]

Although when writing on historical subjects Valle positively

---

[10] The titles of a few of the articles devoted to Valle-Inclán's sources illustrate this point: Corpus Barga, "Valle-Inclán y D'Annunzio"; Pierre Darmangeat, "Valle-Inclán y Barbey d'Aurevilly"; E. S. Speratti Piñero, "Valle-Inclán y un hai-ku de Basho"; J. Sarrailh, "Notes sur Stendhal et Valle-Inclán"; P.P. Rogers, "Mérimée and Valle-Inclán again".

[11] "Valle-Inclán y Ciro Bayo", *NRFH*, XIV (1960), 80.

[12] "Las fuentes de Valle-Inclán", *Simpatías y diferencias* (4ta. serie, Madrid, 1923), 84.

avoided mere chronicling, he tended, none the less, to document himself very well on the historical period which concerned him. In 1909, when engaged in writing the *Carlist War* trilogy, the author decided to visit Navarre which at that time was unknown to him. Valle felt he could not complete a trilogy of novels about the second Carlist War without visiting the area where the Pretender had established his headquarters, and in which so many of the encounters between *facciosos* and *liberales* had taken place. María Dolores Lado gives the following account of his visit:

> Finalmente en 1909, un año más tarde de la aparición de la primera novela carlista, decide ir a buscar en la misma Navarra el ambiente que no puede encontrar en los libros . . . Movido de profunda emoción va siguiendo Valle las viejas rutas carlistas y admirando la grandeza del paisaje navarro. Un día confiesa a su amigo: " —Si hubiera venido antes, querido Argamasilla, le habría dado otro ambiente a *Los cruzados*".[13]

Again, when it came to starting the *Ruedo ibérico* cycle, Valle assimilated a considerable quantity of historical material, including eye-witness accounts, periodicals and histories of the period. According to Gaspar Gómez de la Serna, who has made a close study of Valle's sources for this cycle of novels, the author consulted close on one hundred volumes before embarking on his personal interpretation of the last year of Isabel's reign.[14] Thus it comes as no surprise to discover that although Tierra Caliente is an imaginary state, names, incidents and characters within the novel have a factual or historical basis.

In a letter to Alfonso Reyes written in 1923, Valle mentions that for his portrayal of Santos Banderas he has drawn on a number of Latin-American dictators in order to form a composite character. He writes: "Estos tiempos trabajaba en una novela americana: *Tirano*

---

[13]*Las guerras carlistas y el reinado isabelino en la obra de Ramón del Valle-Inclán* (Gainesville, Florida, 1966), 11.

[14]*España en sus episodios nacionales* (Madrid, 1954), 61-2.

Banderas. La novela de un tirano con rasgos del Doctor Francia, de Rosas, de Melgarejo, de López, y de don Porfirio."[15] In the same letter Valle refers to Roque Cepeda, the antithesis of the Tyrant within the novel, saying that this character is modelled to some extent on Savanarola, although he bears a closer resemblance to the Mexican patriot, Francisco Madero. He also asks Reyes for information about a woman called Teresa Urrea, a controversial figure in Mexico at the time of his first visit to that country in 1891. It is obvious that in 1923 he planned to incorporate "Santa Teresita de Cabora," as she was known, into his projected novel. Later he must have changed his mind since there is no character in *Tirano Banderas* who is even faintly like her. Indeed, between 1923 and 1926 Valle must have made several drastic alterations, because he also writes: "Trazo un gran cataclismo como el terremoto de Valparaíso . . ." and there is no reference to a disaster of this kind in the novel.

A number of critics have studied Valle-Inclán's sources for *Tirano Banderas,* but the essential points are to be found in Emma Speratti's *La elaboración artística en Tirano Banderas.* What follows is a summary of her findings.

Valle availed himself of two chronicles concerning the rebellion of the 'tyrant' Lope de Aguirre against the King of Spain, Philip II. They are Toribio de Ortiguera's *Jornada del río Marañón* and the *Relación verdadera de todo lo que sucedió en la jornada de Omagua y Dorado,* attributed to Francisco Vázquez. Emma Speratti stresses the importance of the chronicles in the elaboration of the novel, and the peculiar skill shown by the author who used them as a springboard for his imagination:

> Las crónicas son uno de los ejes principales y un semillero de sugestiones para distintos episodios y momentos del relato. Valle-

[15]All the quotations from this letter are taken from Emma Speratti's *La elaboración artística en Tirano Banderas* (México, 1957), 147.

Inclán las emplea con esa extraña habilidad suya de labrador de mosaicos, que esta vez se advierte en el ajuste y acomodación de situaciones a una idea fundamentalmente artística, a la cual no es extraña la "síntesis de América".[16]

Three important characters in the novel bear a resemblance to characters described in the chronicles. They are Domiciano de la Gándara, Filomeno Cuevas and the Tyrant himself. Domiciano de la Gándara is modelled on Enrique de Orellana, one of Aguirre's comrades. According to both chronicles, Aguirre orders Orellana's death "porque le dijeron que el día antes se había emborrachado". Evidently there is a very close parallel here, since in the novel Tirano Banderas orders the arrest of Domiciano de la Gándara because the Colonel, in a drunken state, damages some goods belonging to a stall-keeper. Orellana seeks refuge with the Spanish loyalists. In their camp he is greeted with the same suspicion which Domiciano is to encounter when he reaches the home of Filomeno Cuevas. One final similarity refers to the last encounter between tyrant and former friend when the downfall of Aguirre is imminent. In the *Jornada del río Marañón*, Pedro de Orellana encourages Lope de Aguirre's followers to desert him. The same is true of Domiciano at the close of *Tirano Bánderas*: ". . . antes de abrir el fuego, salió de las filas, sobre un buen caballo, el Coronelito de la Gándara. Y corriendo el campo a riesgo de su vida, daba voces intimando la rendición" (829).

Filomeno Cuevas is modelled on a character in the *Jornada del río Marañón* called Pedro Monguía. Valle has been selective and creative in his interpretation of this character since in the original text he was one of Aguirre's followers. However, Filomeno's expedition to Punta de las Serpientes by boat bears many resemblances to a similar one made by Monguía. For example, in the chronicle Monguía has a "negro piloto" —the same being true of Filomeno and

---

[16]*La elaboración artística en Tirano Banderas,* 12.

his party; they arrive at a place called "la Tierra Firme" and, lastly, Lope de Aguirre plans to rendezvous with Monguía at Punta de las Piedras. This place-name no doubt inspired Valle to devise the much more imaginative Punta de las Serpientes on which he places the capital of his imaginary country: "Santa Fe de Tierra Firme —arenales, pitas, manglares, chumberas— en las cartas antiguas, Punta de las Serpientes" (676).

Emma Speratti notes that Valle relied even more heavily on the two chronicles in his depiction of Santos Banderas. For a start, both chronicles refer to Lope de Aguirre as a diabolic character. Valle-Inclán, interested from his earliest writings in witchcraft and satanism, was bound to respond to this facet of Aguirre's character. He does not give it that much prominence but it is brought out, for example, through the fear Niño Santos arouses in the Indians:

> ¡Tenían pacto! ¡Generalito Banderas se proclamaba inmune para las balas por una firma de Satanás! Ante aquel poder tenebroso, invisible y en vela, la plebe cobriza revivía un terror teológico, una fatalidad religiosa poblada de espantos (788).

From the *Relación verdadera* one learns that Lope de Aguirre enjoyed punishing offenders by shaving off their beards. Tirano Banderas also delights in such humiliations, threatening at one point to have a man's hair shorn by his barber, Don Cruz (825).

Emma Speratti thinks that it is in the novel's epilogue that Valle has followed most faithfully the account given by the two chroniclers. She lists the following points of contact: Lope de Aguirre is deserted by some of his most trusted followers; this provokes savage reprisals on his part. He considers escaping but is persuaded to stand his ground. When Aguirre sees his position is desperate he stabs his daughter to death. Later he is shot by the rebels who then proceed to quarter his corpse as a warning to all concerned.

Emma Speratti concludes that in his use and transmutation of these chronicles, Valle reveals himself as a consummate artist. They have served to kindle his imagination, and a comparison of passages from the chronicles and their equivalents in *Tirano Banderas* sheds considerable light on the artistic process involved. One example of this subtle modification of the original texts is provided by the treatment of Lope de Aguirre's daughter. In the *Jornada del río Marañón* we are told merely that she is a beautiful young woman. In Valle's novel this character becomes a pathetic, demented creature who provokes her father's wrath when she escapes from her attendants, thus interrupting his conversation with her wild shrieks:

> Torva y esquiva, aguzados los ojos como montés alimaña, penetró, dando gritos, una mujer encamisada y pelona. Por la sala pasó un silencio, y los coloquios quedaron en el aire (713).

b) *Genesis*

In scene XIV of *Luces de bohemia* there is a long dialogue in a cemetery between the poet Rubén Darío and Valle's *alter ego* the Marqués de Bradomín. Bradomín notices that Darío has jotted down a few lines on the back on an envelope. Having established that this is verse, the Marquis asks if he might see it, but Darío refuses this request because the lines are as yet unpublished. This prompts the Marquis to say:

> Querido Rubén, los versos debieran publicarse con todo su proceso, desde lo que usted llama monstruo hasta la manera definitiva. Tendrían entonces un valor como las pruebas de aguafuerte (I, 952).

Here Valle is giving expression to his own views on the genesis of a work of literature: in a succession of drafts the composition undergoes a series of modifications and improvements until finally the author is satisfied with his work. Valle-Inclán wrote in this manner throughout his literary career and, as Bradomín implies, he was also in the habit of publishing independently 'monstruos' or sketches of works in progress. Some examples of the application of this method will help to illustrate the point.

William Fichter has shown how certain descriptive passages in the *Sonata de estío* (1903), can be traced back through the short story "La niña Chole" (1893) to the early article "Bajo los trópicos. 1. En el mar" published in Mexico in 1892.[17] Emma Speratti has rendered a similar service in helping us to understand the genesis of the *Sonata de otoño*.[18] In her article she considers various episodes later incorporated into the novel. These episodes had first appeared in the magazine *Juventud* and in *El Imparcial* a few months before the publication of the *Sonata* itself. A further example is provided by the short story "Adega" which, widened in scope, was to become *Flor de santidad* (1904).

Valle employed this same method of gradually elaborating relatively simple material with regard to a very different kind of narrative, namely his account of the situation at the French front when he visited Alsace and Champagne in 1916. The substance of his experiences is recorded initially in letters to a personal friend in Spain, and in notebooks where he jotted down his impressions. The scope of the original notes is subsequently broadened in a series of articles written for *El Imparcial* from October 1916 to February 1917. These in turn were to form the basis for *La media noche* (1917).

The genesis of the *Ruedo ibérico* cycle follows the same familiar pattern, although in more complex form, as is to be expected in the case of an ambitious and unfinished cycle of novels. Valle published independently sections of *La corte de los milagros, Viva mi dueño* and *Baza de espadas,* recasting his material before inserting it in one of the novels of the cycle. In a review of *Viva mi dueño* (1928), Gómez de Baquero dwells on the importance of the early drafts in the evolution of this particular novel: "Los episodios sueltos que ha publicado Valle-Inclán en periódicos, no son capítulos desprendidos

[17]"Sobre la génesis de la *Sonata de estío*", *NRFH,* VII (1953), 526-535.
[18]"Génesis y evolución de la *Sonata de otoño*", *RHM,* XXV (1959), 57-80.

del libro, sino apuntes, estudios o esbozos que permiten entrever la elaboración artística."[19]

Predictably, the genesis of *Tirano Banderas* follows the lines of the works already described. Here, as is the case with the *Sonata de otoño*, it is Emma Speratti who has successfully traced its development. Four chapters of the future novel were published independently in the June-July and December issues of the magazine *El estudiante* in 1925, and in the January-February number of 1926. The chapters in question were "El jueguito de la rana", "El honorable cuerpo diplomático", "Mitote revolucionario" and "La mueca verde". *Zacarías el cruzado o agüero nigromante* was published in the collection *La novela de hoy* in September 1926. The completed novel appeared in the same year. Here too, the early drafts show that modifications and improvements were made before the material was inserted into the body of the novel.

Emma Speratti comments on obvious changes in the structure of *Tirano Banderas*, changes which she attributes to "un nuevo concepto de lo que debía ser el conjunto de la obra". My own opinion is that this new conception of the novel is related to Valle's desire to use number symbolism in the structure. The order in which the books appear in *El estudiante* differs from that of the final version. This change of position is not arbitrary, since in their original order events followed one another in a rather mechanical fashion. The re-distribution of 'scenes' and chapters adds an element of surprise which Emma Speratti equates with the rapid scene-shifts of a film-camera.

There are times when Valle adds material to a certain scene to clarify the development of the action, as in scene five of "El juego de la ranita". Here hints are dropped about the Tyrant's plan to

[19]"Letras e ideas: *Viva mi dueño*", *El Sol*, 1 November 1928, 1.

interrupt a political meeting at the Harris Circus and, at the same time, more light is shed on his character. The reader is shown the duplicity which permits the Tyrant simultaneously to persuade Don Celes to visit the Spanish Minister and to persevere with the enquiries which, he trusts, will prevent any action on the part of the Diplomatic Corps. With the same end in view, a very brief introduction describing the Spanish Club is inserted at the beginning of the chapter entitled "Cuarzos ibéricos". Valle probably added these lines because without them the beginning would have appeared rather abrupt and possibly puzzled the reader. Indeed, these brief descriptions in the manner of stage directions, which appear at the start of a new chapter or section, are a feature of the novel as a whole.

Other changes are of a practical order: they are not designed to convey more information but to convey it in a more striking fashion. Words may be added, suppressed, their order altered or they may be discarded in favour of synonyms to create a more vivid or rhythmical effect. Here are some examples from both the earlier and definitive versions which show the care Valle took to find the *mot juste*:

Te devolveré la tumbaguita. No hago cuenta de los bolivianos. Recoge esos restos. Dales sepultura ... (*Zac.*, 58)

Te devolveré la tumbaguita. No hago caso de los bolivianos. ¡Quiere decirse que te beneficias con mi plata! Recoge esos restos. Dales sepultura ... (*T.B.*, 766)

Here, the addition of Quintín Pereda's wheedling plea shows how he judges others according to his own lights, believing them as grasping as he is.

Santa Fe, con una furia trágica y devoradora del tiempo, escapaba de su sueño de pesadilla, con el grito de sus ferias, luminoso y tumultuoso como un grito bélico ("El honorable cuerpo diplomático", 6)

Santa Fe, con una furia trágica y devoradora del tiempo, escapaba *del terrorífico sopor cotidiano*, con el grito de sus ferias, tumultuoso como un grito bélico (*T.B.*, 688)

In this case, the rather well-worn words, "sueño de pesadilla", give way to the more original and therefore striking "terrorífico sopor cotidiano".

It is also typical of the *esperpento* aesthetic that certain neutral words employed in the first draft should be replaced in the final version by expressions which serve to dehumanise characters. An example of this is provided by a description of the Spanish Minister who, in the original draft, is described as "estirando la pierna con leve cojera". In *Tirano Banderas* the unemotive *pierna* is replaced by *zanca* (shank or animal's leg).

In terms of its genesis, as in many other respects, *Tirano Banderas* marks no departure from the rest of Valle-Inclán's works. The emphasis on craftsmanship is as much in evidence here as elsewhere. The painstaking method used in the elaboration of this and other novels shows how in Valle's case inspiration counted for far less than conscious artistry.

IV

The Esperpento

¡No os lo merecíais!   ¡Ya me he cansado!
¡Ahora arte de feria, barraca y aleluya!

The first and fullest definition of the *esperpento* is to be found in *Luces de bohemia*, an armchair play published in the journal *La Pluma* in 1920. Valle provides more detail in the prologue to *Los cuernos de don Friolera* which appeared in the same magazine a year later. However, a number of features which characterize the *esperpento* are present in much earlier works although only in random or attenuated form. These earlier works lack the acerbity which informs most of Valle's later production.

The word *esperpento* is applied to something freakish and ugly.[20] It means, in short, a 'fright'. In *Luces de bohemia*, Valle-Inclán states that Spain is a "deformación grotesca de la civilización europea" (I, 939), and that the tragic sense of Spanish life can only be rendered accurately by an aesthetic posited on systematic or mathematical distortion. The characters who figure in the *esperpentos* are human beings as reflected in distorting mirrors. It follows that these grotesque beings are not sympathetically treated by the author. They all have equal status in the inchoate, topsy-turvy world of the *esperpento*.

It has been said that the true *esperpentos* are those in dramatic form and which are concerned strictly with urban environments. If these criteria are applied, the *esperpento* genre is reduced to the three plays in the collection *Martes de carnaval* (1930) and *Luces de bohemia* itself. But it proves fruitless and sterile to impose demarc-

---

[20]Martín Alonso, in his *Enciclopedia del idioma* (Madrid, 1958), II, 1854, defines the word as a "persona o cosa notable por su fealdad o mala traza. Desatino, absurdo".

ation lines, because the spirit of the *esperpento* informs everything Valle wrote from roughly 1920 until his death in 1936. It is not surprising therefore that when questioned about the characters in the novels he was engaged on writing in the 1920's he should have described them as "enanos que juegan una tragedia", adding:

> Vienen a ser estas novelas [*Tirano Banderas* and the *Ruedo ibérico* cycle] *esperpentos* acrecidos y trabajados con elementos que no podían darse en la forma dramática de *Luces de bohemia* y de *Los cuernos de don Friolera.*[21]

Thus Valle explains why he turned his attention away from drama to a genre which offered him greater scope and freedom. But it must not be forgotten that although these novels are on a larger scale than the plays, they remain *esperpentos*. Both the characters and the atmosphere in which they move are similar to, say, *Los cuernos de don Friolera*. It remains now to define this spirit and to see how it is reflected in *Tirano Banderas.*

As long as Valle-Inclán adhered to the tenets of *Modernismo*, he both ignored and disdained the society of his own times, taking refuge in a brittle, artificial world of his own devising. The milieux in which his characters moved were either aristocratic or archaic and the author carefully avoided reference to anything pedestrian or squalid. Even aspects of life such as war or murder, normally considered brutal or degrading, were idealised so as to harmonise with the refinement of the whole. As Valle matured he found it increasingly difficult to ignore the more sordid and distressing aspects of the society in which he lived. Initially, in plays such as the *Farsa de la cabeza del dragón* (1914) and *La marquesa Rosalinda* (1913), there are only intimations of a change in outlook. This is reflected in the style, the treatment of characters and the satirical comments aimed at various aspects of Spanish society such as the

---

[21] G. Martínez Sierra, "Hablando con Valle-Inclán: de él y de su obra", *ABC*, 7 December 1928.

incompetence of the Crown and the outdated concern with reputa-ion and honour. However, at this stage, Valle's satire is by no means as vitriolic as it was to become in the *esperpentos*.

With the passage of time Valle's mood became angrier and the mood is matched by a language whose rhythm is jerky and full of discordant notes. Slang and dialect terms, verbal crudities, grotesque effects derived from the juxtaposition of noble and base terms, all these commingle to form a style of great richness and originality which reflects very accurately his attitude to the society of the period. Valle's standpoint emerges in a number of ways. One of these is based on the belief that modern man, unlike his forefathers, is not equipped to deal with tragic circumstances:

> Los hombres son distintos, minúsculos, para sostener ese gran peso. De ahí nace el contraste, la desproporción, lo ridículo. El dolor de Don Friolera es el mismo que el de Otelo, y, sin embargo, no tiene su grandeza. La ceguera es bella y noble en Homero. Pero en *Luces de bohemia* esa misma ceguera es triste y lamentable porque se trata de un poeta bohemio: de Máximo Estrella . . .[22]

Just as Max Estrella is the latter-day equivalent of Homer, and the pathetic Friolera the twentieth century's answer to Othello, so Juanito Ventolera in the *esperpento Las galas del difunto* is the modern equivalent of the dashing Don Juan, and Isabel II a caricature of an earlier Spanish queen, her namesake Isabel I. This feature, common to a number of Valle-Inclán's works of the twenties, does not appear in *Tirano Banderas*, for it is not the author's intention to present Santos Banderas as a caricature of some earlier leader of men. Instead, as I have already mentioned, he draws on what might be termed a Latin-American rogue's gallery of dictators to fashion this particular character. *Tirano Banderas* also differs from many of the remaining *esperpento* works in that it does not include blistering

[22] These lines are from an interview with José Montero Alonso. Extracts from this interview preface *Otra castiza de Samaria* (an early draft of sections from *Baza de espadas*). It was published in Madrid in 1929 in the collection *La novela de hoy*.

assaults on the army. The explanation for this is simple: Valle's anger was directed exclusively at the Spanish army and there could be no outlet for it in Tierra Caliente.

In nearly every other respect *Tirano Banderas* is a typical product of Valle-Inclán's maturity. It includes the satire of sentimental, maudlin fiction and vacuous grandiloquence which is so much to the fore in *Los cuernos de don Friolera* and the novels of the *Ruedo ibérico* cycle. Stylistically too there are few differences between this and other works of the same period. There is the predictable rich assortment of dehumanising metaphors, the same jerky rhythm, the same stylisation of both characters and background, the same degree of concision. The language, it is true, does differ from that of other works of the period in that here Valle is attempting to create a common tongue for all Hispanic people by incorporating words used in different parts of Spanish America. However, this is not really a major difference, since in the *esperpento* plays and the *Ruedo ibérico* cycle the language is enriched by the use of gypsies' cant and slang terms. In addition, there is a fairly strong injection of Spanish-American words in these works owing to the presence of 'indianos' and army officers who have done service in Cuba.

The attitude to the characters in *Tirano Banderas* does not depart markedly from the *esperpento*'s norm, although more admiration and compassion are shown here towards a minority of Creoles and Indians. Valle's treatment of the remainder, that is the majority, is the remote god-like one characteristic of the *esperpento* period. He described this detached attitude as "una superación del dolor y de la risa, como deben ser las conversaciones de los muertos al contarse historias de los vivos" (I, 992-93). In terms of themes, cruelty, violence and death are as integral to *Tirano Banderas* as to Valle-Inclán's other works of this period. Indeed, in this respect there is little point in distinguishing between earlier and later works since these themes engrossed his attention from the very start.

V

The Major Themes

a) *Death*

Two themes are of fundamental importance in *Tirano Banderas*: death and society. Of these, death —almost invariably accompanied by cruelty and violence— is by far the more important. Whether one chooses to give a curt summary of the action or to linger over the smallest details, it proves impossible to avoid this dominating theme.

For a start, the choice of the two days on which the bulk of the action takes place cannot be without significance. The festivals of All Saints and All Souls are particularly important in Mexico, a country which, as Octavio Paz has pointed out, both disdains and is fascinated by death:

> El desprecio a la muerte no está reñido con el culto que le profesamos . . . La fascinación que ejerce sobre nosotros quizá brote de nuestro hermetismo y de la furia con que lo rompemos . . . Cuando estallamos, tocamos el punto más alto de la tensión, rozamos el vértice vibrante de la vida. Y allí, en la altura del frenesí, sentimos el vértigo: La muerte nos atrae.[23]

It is interesting to note the similarities between Paz's remarks and Valle's description of the revelries in the town:

> Santa Fe se regocijaba con un vértigo encendido, con una calentura de luz y tinieblas . . . Sentíase la oscura y desolada palpitación de la vida sobre la fosa abierta. Santa Fe, con una furia trágica y devoradora del tiempo, escapaba del terrorífico sopor cotidiano con el grito de sus ferias, tumultuoso como un grito bélico (688).

These two passages are linked not only by the use of identical words such as *furia* and *vértigo*, but also by their demonstration that life in its moments of maximum intensity brings us that much closer to death.

---

[23] *El laberinto de la soledad* (México, 1959), 52.

The lives of Tierra Caliente's inhabitants depend on the whim of one man, Santos Banderas, who is himself but a symbol of death. The connection is established from the first moment this character is introduced: Don Santos has just returned from Zamalpoa where he has savagely crushed an uprising against his régime. The association between Tirano Banderas and death is presented in a number of ways. The Tyrant controls the lives of the citizens in a completely arbitrary way and is not characterised by compassion for his fellows. Nachite, the Tyrant's buffoon, asks an old revolutionary in the fortress prison of Santa Mónica if he has been sentenced to death. The prisoner replies with a shrug: "¿ Pues conoce otra penalidad más clemente el Tigre de Zamalpoa?" (774)

Towards the novel's end Santos Banderas gives full rein to his brutal instincts. He orders fifteen of his soldiers to be hanged as an example to their comrades who, in his opinion, are not showing enough zeal in his defence. At the same time he orders the death of the Indian who has been left half-buried near the parade ground after being lashed. This is a purely gratuitous killing, carried out merely to ensure he is not released by the revolutionaries. The bloodshed caused by the Tyrant is ended only by his own violent death. Under the circumstances it is hardly surprising that the people should extract some measure of revenge by having his corpse decapitated, quartered and displayed in the four principal towns of the land.

The sadistic cruelty of Tirano Banderas extends to his minions. For example, there is a dark legend about the governor of Santa Mónica: "El . . . Coronel Irineo Castañón, aparece en las relaciones de aquel tiempo como uno de los más crueles sicarios de la Tiranía . . ." (771). Even an insignificant incident, as when one of the Tyrant's henchmen splits a coconut with a knife, serves to stress the character's vein of primitive cruelty: "El Mayor Abilio del Valle, que se preciaba de haber cortado muchas cabezas, pidió la gracia de meter el facón a los mosquitos de agua" (691).

Don Santos, at the hub of this dark world, is consistently described by images of death:

> . . . parecía una calavera con antiparras negras y corbatín de clérigo (676).

> . . . cruzaba la cera de las manos (691).

> La momia amarilla desplegó las manos (691).

Some of the minor characters, too, are repeatedly associated with the macabre. This is true of the pallid young girl who earns a meagre living for herself and her blind father by singing while the latter accompanies her at the piano:

> La chamaca fúnebre pasaba la bandejilla . . . (722)

> La amortajada puso los tristes ojos en una estrella (723).

> Cantaba la chicuela, tirante las cuerdas del triste descote, inmóvil la cara de niña muerta, el fúnebre resplandor de la bandejilla del petitorio sobre el pecho (717).

Another minor character constantly presented in terms of macabre images is Bernardino Arias, one of Nachito's companions at cards in the fortress of Santa Mónica.[24] The inmates of the prison can never escape the presence of death, which they await not only with resignation but with pride. Borne on the waves that break against the prison walls is a row of putrefying corpses —those of their former comrades. The sharks, as one inmate observes cynically, are glutted on revolutionary flesh.

Reminders of death are always in the background: the buzzards circling overhead; the allusions to the monastery of San Martín de los Mostenses, the Tyrant's headquarters; the number of ill-omens and the crude murals on the monastery wall when the Tyrant is signing a death warrant: "Sobre la cal de los muros, daban sus espantos malas pinturas de martirios, purgatorios, catafalcos y demonios verdes" (710-11). Even the clay bells fashioned by the natives are described as "fúnebres barros" (715). The novel is nothing more

---

[24] See pp. 781, 782 & 784.

than a symphony of death:

> El tumbo del mar batía la muralla, y el oboe de las olas cantaba el triunfo de la muerte. Los pájaros negros hacían círculos en el remoto azul, y sobre el losado del patio se pintaba la sombra fugitiva del aleteo (775).

Furthermore, death is no longer depicted as noble, beautiful or even decorative as it had been previously in Valle's *modernista* phase. It is a grotesque carnival death, a macabre farce, to which Nachito's description provides the key: "La mengua de aquel bufón en desgracia tenía cierta solemnidad grotesca, como los entierros de mojiganga con que fina el antruejo" (777).

b) *Society*

In his depiction of Tierra Caliente and its society, Valle-Inclán has succeeded in creating a state which is representative of Latin America as a whole. However, this statement requires two qualifications. The first of these is that the social organisation of Tierra Caliente is appropriate only to the subcontinent's more backward countries, chiefly to those with a large percentage of Amerindian inhabitants. Consequently it has little if any bearing on countries such as Argentina, Uruguay and Chile. The second qualification is that for reasons which are readily explained, Tierra Caliente and its dictator bear a closer resemblance to the Mexico of Porfirio Díaz than to any other Latin-American state.

Porfirio Díaz was dictator of Mexico from 1876 to 1911.[25] His régime, like Santos Banderas', was ended by a revolution, although he did not meet the violent death Valle ascribes to his Tyrant. Porfirio Díaz too was of Indian extraction and professed the same indifference to those of his own race as does Santos Banderas in Valle's novel.[26]

---

[25] Granted that *Tirano Banderas* is set in 1873, there is a slight inconsistency in dates. This is unlikely to have troubled Valle-Inclán owing to his scorn of realism and its trappings.

[26] "Díaz, despite his Indian blood, had little faith in the indigenous peoples of

Furthermore, Díaz, like Valle's Tyrant, had to face increasing resistance from workers in the last years of his dictatorship. Strikes were organised in various parts of Mexico and these, in Hubert Herring's words, were "bloodily crushed by Díaz's efficient *rurales*". This brings to mind the suppression of the Zamalpoa rebellion at the very start of *Tirano Banderas*.

Díaz was notorious for his policy of welcoming foreign investors without due regard to the claims of national sovereignty and prosperity. Mexico's economic situation under Díaz is summarised by Hubert Herring as follows:

> Foreign capital was thus welcomed by Díaz until it dominated the economic life of the nation. The Americans and the British owned oil wells and mines. The French controlled most of the growing textile business and many of the large shops. The Germans controlled the trade in hardware and drugs. The Spaniards (and especially the *gallegos* from Galicia) were grocers and other retail merchants. . . The Mexicans, untrained in modern techniques, were, in effect, aliens in their own land.

In Tierra Caliente, as in Porfirio's Mexico, the foreign investor is very much to the fore, although it is interesting to note that the author, faithful to his *patria chica*, includes no Galicians among the wicked *gachupines*.[27]

Also relevant in this context are a few details of Valle-Inclán's life. The author was well acquainted with Mexico, having visited it on two occasions. In his youth he spent the better part of a year in Mexico, and was there in 1892 when Porfirio Díaz was at the height of his power. Valle's second visit to Mexico was made in 1921 when he was invited by President Obregón to attend the independence

Mexico" (Hubert Herring, *A History of Latin America*, London, 1968, 330). Subsequent quotations from Herring are taken from pp. 336 and 331.

[27] Teodosio del Araco, a Spanish landowner, comes from Alava; Cucarachita, who owns a brothel, hails from Cadiz; Quintín Pereda is a native of Asturias; and the editor of the local Spanish newspaper, Nicolás Díaz del Rivero, is Aragonese. Don Celes Galindo's place of origin is not mentioned.

festivities in Mexico City. During this, his second stay in Mexico, Valle aroused the hostility of the Spanish community by stating openly that he was in favour of agrarian reform. The author's acquaintance with other Latin-American states was slight, amounting to brief glimpses of Argentina, Paraguay, Bolivia and Chile when he accompanied his wife, the actress Josefina Blanco, on a tour with the theatrical company of María Guerrero in 1910. *Tirano Banderas* could also be interpreted as an expression of gratitude on Valle's part for the hospitality extended to him by President Obregón.

The Indian population of Tierra Caliente almost always forms the base of the social pyramid. The few exceptions to this rule have no sympathy for their downtrodden fellows. The Indians are generally passive and mute, "soturnos en la cruel indiferencia del dolor y de la muerte" (676). They provide the landowners with a large labour force which is exploited to the maximum. However, they are capable of rebelling against their lot as is demonstrated not only by Zacarías el Cruzado but, in addition, by a very minor character called Indalecio Santana. Santana gives the following description of his past life when imprisoned in Santa Mónica:

> Nací en la Hacienda de Chamulpo. Allí nací, pero todavía chamaco me trasladaron con una reata de peones a los Llanos de Zamalpoa. Cuando estalló la bola revolucionaria, desertamos todos los peones de las minas de un judas gachupín y nos fuimos con Doroteo (786).[28]

Valle's sympathy for the Mexican Indian was unquestionably sincere,[29] and the championing of an entire section of the community is unique in the literature of the *esperpento*.

---

[28]Doroteo Rojas was the leader of a guerrilla band.

[29]In this context it is worth quoting an extract from a poem by Valle entitled "Nos vemos", published in *México Moderno* on September 1, 1922:
> ¡Indio mexicano que la encomienda tornó mendigo!
> ¡Indio mexicano!
> ¡Rebélate y quema las trojes del trigo!
> ¡Rebélate hermano!

Higher up the social pyramid one finds a colourful assortment of people: poor whites like El Ciego Velones and his daughter; prostitutes, street vendors and members of the middle class like the student Marco Aurelio Pintado who is unjustly incarcerated in Santa Mónica. All these characters play a subsidiary rôle in the proceedings. Above them are those who have money or influence: the *gachupines,* all of whom are corrupt, a small number of Indians, and the educated creoles. It is understandable, granted his nationality, that of the various countries involved in despoiling Tierra Caliente, Valle-Inclán should direct most of his criticism at the Spanish. Close to the beginning of the first part, the reader is given this cutting description of a cross-section of the Spanish community:

> Niño Santos se retiró de la ventana para recibir a una endomingada diputación de la Colonia Española. El abarrotero, el empeñista, el chulo del braguetazo, el patriota jactancioso, el doctor sin reválida, el periodista hampón, el rico mal afamado, se inclinaban en hilera ante la momia taciturna ... (677-8)

The condemnation of Spanish society to be found in the *Ruedo ibérico* novels is reflected in the bitter satire of those Spaniards who figure in *Tirano Banderas*. However, this does not mean that, as Emma Speratti supposes, Valle is concerned here chiefly with Spain.[30]

There is no general description of the creoles to match that of the Spanish community, so one is obliged to form one's own conclusions based upon the few characters in the novel who belong to this social class. If one excepts the politician Sánchez Ocaña, who is ridiculed by the author, the remainder, that is, Filomeno Cuevas, Roque Cepeda and the writer Dr Atl, are all treated sympathetically by the author. It is from this quarter that the Indian's redemption and the creation

---

[30] According to this critic: "*Tirano Banderas* es la interpretación en América de un problema español: la presencia repetida e insistente del *Espadón* que se opone al buen deseo democrático" (*La elaboración artística en Tirano Banderas,* 128). One should not forget that the military dictator is also, very obviously, "un problema americano", and that when Valle wished to satirise the Spanish army he used Spain as his backcloth.

of a more equitable society is likely to come. But it should be added that for Valle the future of Tierra Caliente would appear uncertain: this reflects the pessimistic view of mankind he expressed in the following letter to Cipriano Rivas Cherif written in 1923:

> Trabajo en una novela americana de caudillaje y avaricia gachu-pinesca . . . Creo cada día con mayor fuerza que el hombre no se gobierna por sus ideas ni por su cultura. Imagino un fatalismo del medio, de la herencia y de las taras fisiológicas, siendo la conducta totalmente desprendida de los pensamientos. Y, en cambio, siendo los oscuros pensamientos motrices, consecuencia de las fatalidades del medio, herencia y salud. Solo el orgullo del hombre le hace suponer que es un animal pensante.[31]

On the periphery of this society, yet affecting it indirectly, are the members of the Diplomatic Corps. Of these the only one who is given considerable prominence is the Spanish Minister. Initially Tirano Banderas fears diplomatic interference in national affairs. It has reached his ears that the diplomats have objected to the shooting of prisoners taken at Zamalpoa and that they plan to hold a meeting about this incident to be followed by an official protest. It turns out that Santos Banderas has seriously overestimated their moral courage and capacity for reaching clear-cut decisions. The sum total of the diplomats' deliberations is summarised by Valle with cutting irony. The passage in question serves as an excellent example of what Julián Marías terms the "comentario intrínseco":

> Tras prolija discusión se redactó una nota. La firmaban veinti-siete Naciones. Fue un acto transcendental. El suceso, troquelado con el estilo epigráfico y lacónico del cable, rodó por los grandes periódicos del mundo: "Santa Fe de Tierra Firme. El Honorable Cuerpo Diplomático acordó la presentación de una nota al Gobierno de la República. La nota, a la cual se atribuye gran importancia, aconseja el cierre de los expendios de bebidas y exige el refuerzo de guardias en las Legaciones y Bancos Extranjeros" (808-09).

Whilst Valle could see virtues in the Indians and the creoles, the

[31] Quoted by David Lagmanovich, in "La visión de América en *Tirano Banderas*", *Humanitas* (Tucumán), III (1955), 275.

members of the Diplomatic Corps are all dehumanised, trivial creatures. They are typical figures of the *esperpento* period who are treated with no respect whatsoever by the author.

Tierra Caliente is, thus, typical of the more backward Latin-American states, as much in terms of its economic dependence on foreign capital as of its social divisions. However, I hope I have shown that for understandable reasons Tierra Caliente and its tyrant are modelled to a considerable extent on the Mexico of Porfirio Díaz and the revolution which ended his régime in 1911. In this context it is amusing to note that Zacarías' dog is called Porfirio.

VI

The Principal Characters

The symmetrical arrangement of the various sections of *Tirano Banderas* is echoed by the balance and precision with which the central characters are disposed. Here again, as Valle indicated in an interview with Gregorio Martínez Sierra, three is an all-important digit:

> En cuanto a la trama, pensé que América está constituída por el indio, por el criollo y por el extranjero. Al indio que tanto es allí alguna vez presidente como de ordinario paria, lo desenvolví en tres figuras: Generalito Banderas, el paria que sufre el duro castigo del chicote, y el indio del plagio y la bola revolucionaria, Zacarías el Cruzado.[32]

Valle adds that the three creoles are Filomeno Cuevas, Sánchez Ocaña and Roque Cepeda. The Spanish residents are represented by Don Celes, Baron Benicarlés and the pawnbroker, Quintín Pereda. Thus the emphasis laid on the number 3 in the novel's structure is repeated in the study of society: three racial and social groups are considered, each one studied through three characters.

There can be no argument as to the identity of the most important character in this novel. The title alone makes this abundantly clear. Consequently it is Santos Banderas whom I shall consider first and in the greatest detail. I shall omit any reference to the Indian "que sufre el duro castigo del chicote" because his role is symbolic and we are given no details about his character or circumstances.

The Indian

a) *Santos Banderas*

Not all the characters in *Tirano Banderas* are dehumanised. This is rare in Valle's later works and indicates that the few exceptions are fundamentally good and upright people. Filomeno Cuevas, Zacarías el Cruzado and Roque Cepeda are all spared the grotesque metaphors normally used by the author to strip his characters of their dignity and humanity. However, the Tyrant is more intensely and consistently dehumanised than any other character. But although Valle never tires of stressing Tirano Banderas' stiff movements, his

[32]*ABC*, 7 December 1928.

corpse-like appearance and his resemblance to a bird of prey, he is not presented as a one-dimensional character. In the course of the novel a number of the Tyrant's facets are considered, facets which are either his by right or with which others have endowed him.

Valle conceives his protagonist as crafty, hypocritical and a skilful politician. He is also pedantic, prudish, ceremonious, merciless, suspicious, sadistic and cynical. He wears dark green glasses, mops his brow with a handkerchief "propio de dómine o donado" and has a thin cracked voice. He chews coca most of the time with the result that there is always a trickle of green spittle at the corners of his mouth. Others regard him as an ominous and inescapable presence.[33] Redeeming features are noticeable by their absence, save that Niño Santos is conscious of the very real threat to his country represented by foreign commercial interests. He resents their interference very deeply:

> El caudillaje criollo, la indiferencia del indígena, la crápula del mestizo y la teocracia colonial son los tópicos con que nos denigran el industrialismo yanqui y las monas de la diplomacia europea. Su negocio está en hacerle la capa a los bucaneros de la revolución, para arruinar nuestros valores y alzarse concesionarios de minas, ferrocarriles y aduanas . . . ¡Vamos a pelearles el gallo sacando de la prisión, con todos los honores, al futuro Presidente de la República! (792)

Of all the characteristics mentioned, the ones to which most space and attention are given are his cruelty and sadism. Part one begins with a curt allusion to the Tyrant's suppression of the Zamalpoa rebellion. This is followed by a description of Santos Banderos watching an Indian being buried in the ground up to the waist before being lashed by two corporals. This incident —like nearly all the

---

[33]For example, Don Celes' peace of mind is disturbed by a sudden vision of the Tyrant: "Y subitánea, en un silo de sombra taciturna, atisbó la mueca de Tirano Banderas" (800). Laurita, the wife of Filomeno Cuevas, equates Tirano Banderas with a menacing deity: ". . . presentía imágenes tumultuosas de la revolución. Muertes, incendios, suplicios y, remota como una divinidad implacable, la momia del Tirano" (768).

others in the novel— is related by the author in a completely detached manner. The same applies to Valle's description of Tirano Banderas when he is relaxing with his henchmen while in the distance a group of revolutionaries are being shot by a firing squad. Here again the author avoids any direct comment on the situation:

> Tirano Banderas, ajeno a la fusilería, cruel y vesánico, afinaba el punto apretando la boca. Los cirrus de humo volaban sobre el mar.
> — ¡Rana!
> El Tirano, siempre austero, vuelto a la trinca de compadres, desplegaba el pañuelo de dómine, enjugándose el cráneo pelado:
> — ¡Aprendan, y no se distraigan del juego con macanas! (689)

Santos Banderas' sadism is brought out in two ways. The first of these is the delight he takes in humiliating one of his more cowardly followers, Nachito Veguillas, by asking him repeatedly to adopt the position of a frog and to imitate its croak. The second is his taunting of the charlatan Dr Polaco who maintains that the young prostitute, Lupita la Romántica, is psychic. Santos Banderas informs Lupita's 'manager' that, considering him a trickster, he will have his head shaved by his barber Don Cruz. The Tyrant's amusement increases when it emerges that Dr Polaco is in any event quite bald (825).

The causes of Santos Banderas' behaviour are implied in Valle's description of him as "cruel y vesánico", and his own mental disturbance is underscored by the fact that his daughter is completely insane:

> Tirano Banderas se acercó a la encamisada, que con el gesto obstinado de los locos, hundía las uñas en la greña y se agazapaba en un rincón aullando:
> —Manolita, vos serés bien mandada. Andate no más para la recámara (714).

The other aspects of the Tyrant's character which are given prominence are his slyness and his puritanism. When he makes overtures of peace to his political opponent, Roque Cepeda, the latter, conscious of his cunning, says bluntly that Don Santos reminds him

of "la serpiente del Génesis" (794). Hypocrisy is also to the forefront when Tirano Banderas grants his political rivals permission to
hold a public meeting at the Circo Harris. This apparently friendly
gesture is belied by the fact that he arranges to have the meeting
interrupted by hecklers and ridiculed by the press.

The protagonist's ascetic way of life is illustrated by some of the
images applied to him, his place of residence and, in addition, by his
reaction to certain incidents in the novel. Chief among these is his
evident disgust when he learns that the Spanish ambassador is a
homosexual. "Aberraciones repugnantes", snorts the Tyrant when
his Chief of Police gives him details about the Spanish baron's affair
with an Andalusian called Currito mi Alma.

Tirano Banderas is not a sybaritic dictator; indeed, his way of life
is frankly austere. One of his few amusements is the game of 'ranita'
about which he remarks primly "no arruina como otros juegos" (682).
As I have already mentioned, some of the images applied to him
underline his puritanical nature:

> . . . masculló estudiadas cláusulas de dómine (678).
> La momia enlevitada respondía con cuáquera dignidad . . . (792).
> El Tirano, raposo y clerical, arrugaba la boca entre sus ayudantes
> lagartijeros (793).
> En la puerta saludó con una cortesía de viejo cuáquero (705).

Valle would appear to connect the bird of prey —nocturnal and
deadly— with the kind of authoritarian religion, harking back to
colonial times, which Tirano Banderas represents. Often he is
described as a "corneja sagrada", a "pájaro sagrado" or a "lechuzo".
It is fitting that the former monastery, San Martín de los Mostenses,
is situated on a hill overlooking the town of Santa Fe, so that the
bird of prey seems to be hovering over its intended victims.

b) *Zacarías el Cruzado*

Zacarías San José, commonly known as 'el Cruzado' owing to a
scar across his face, is one of the few characters in the novel who is
not a caricature of a human being. Much of the pathos and emotion

to be found in *Tirano Banderas* —in truth, very little— is related to this character and the tragic loss of his child.

Zacarías' troubles start when Colonel Domiciano de la Gándara, one of the Tyrant's intimates, falls into disgrace. The vindictive Don Santos orders his immediate arrest on the grounds that Domiciano has been drunk and disorderly. But Domiciano is warned of the danger just in time and is able to escape. He then recalls that Zacarías is indebted to him for past favours and decides to ask for his help. The Indian takes him by boat to the house of Filomeno Cuevas where Domiciano offers his services to the revolutionaries. Domiciano's decision to ask Zacarías for assistance starts a concatenation of events which is to end with Zacarías himself espousing the cause of the rebels.

Domiciano gives Zacarías a quite valuable ring as a token of his gratitude, and before escorting the Colonel to safety he asks his wife to pawn it. The pawnbroker she visits, a Spaniard or *gachupín* called Quintín Pereda, is one of the most malignant characters in the novel. It does not take him long to conclude that an Indian woman is unlikely to have acquired a costly ring by legal means. Therefore he gives her a paltry sum for it and threatens to denounce her to the police if she queries his price. The avaricious pawnbroker then replaces the stone with a cheaper one and takes it to the Tyrant's Chief of Police who congratulates him on his 'civismo'. This results in Zacarías' *chinita* being taken to prison. As she is dragged away from her home she cries out to her little boy to follow her:

— ¡Ven! ¡Corre!
Pero el niño no se movía. Detenido sobre la orilla de la acequia, sollozaba mirando crecer la distancia que le separaba de la madre (735).

When Zacarías returns home he discovers that his small boy has died in a particularly gruesome fashion:

Horrorizado y torvo, levanta un despojo sangriento. ¡Era cuanto encontraba de su chamaco! Los cerdos habían devorado la cara

y las manos del niño: los zopilotes le habían sacado el corazón
del pecho (759).

After brooding for a long time in utter immobility, Zacarías decides
to seek revenge. Once he has placed his son's remains in a bag, the
Indian buys a horse and proceeds to the pawnbroker's shop. There he
encircles the *gachupín*'s neck with a long whip and drags the throttled
corpse over the cobblestones. After avenging his child's death,
Zacarías joins the revolutionaries.

Zacarías is not portrayed as an individual. His being and circumstances are archetypal. All we learn about him is that he is loyal,
determined and far from meek. In addition, he seldom reveals
personal emotion save when on seeing Filomeno's children he observes
simply "Son pidazos del corazón" (769).

It cannot be doubted that Valle-Inclán was sincere in his championing of the underprivileged Indians and in his implicit abhorrence of
the élitist attitude shown towards their fellows by the few Indians
belonging to the ruling classes. It is Tirano Banderas himself who
expresses this scorn towards his own kind when in conversation with
Roque Cepeda: "Usted," he says, "criollo de la mejor prosapia,
reniega del criollismo. Yo en cambio, indio por las cuatro ramas,
descreo de las virtudes y capacidades de mi raza" (814).

In his defence of the Indian serf, Valle expresses the same
political sympathies as when he considers the social structure in
Spain. In political terms Valle-Inclán was a hopeless romantic, hence
throughout his life his sympathies lay with extremists: either the
Anarchists or the Carlists; either the Galician peasant or the genuine
Spanish aristocracy. The latter, so far as he was concerned, were best
represented by the Galician squirearchy. It was the middle strata of
society, the *bourgeoisie* and *petite bourgeoisie,* which Valle could
never stomach, this being as clear in *Tirano Banderas* as elsewhere in
his work. Interestingly enough, however, in his later works about
Spain, the peasants —be they Galician or Andalusian— are seen

through the distorting mirror of the *esperpento*. But in this novel
the Indians form part of a revolutionary epic destined to assert the
rights of the downtrodden. Consequently they are treated like the
Galician beggars of *Romance de lobos* (1908) rather than as the
barbaric peasants of the *Ruedo ibérico*.

The Creole

a) *Filomeno Cuevas*

Filomeno Cuevas emerges as a totally admirable man, both as an
individual and as a leader of men. Endowed with a strong sense of
duty, he discovers that it is impossible for him to ignore the predic-
ament of his fellow-citizens. Action rather than wishful thinking
proves the only salve for his conscience, so he takes up arms against
the tyrant. When Laurita, Filomeno's wife, remonstrates with him
for abandoning their home, he points out to her and his assembled
children that it is a matter of duty:

> He creído hasta ahora que podía ser un buen ciudadano, trabajando
> por acrecentarles la hacienda, sin sacrificar cosa ninguna al
> servicio de la Patria. Pero hoy me acusa mi conciencia, y no
> quiero avergonzarme mañana ni que ustedes se avergüencen de su
> padre (768).

Although Filomeno is an upright and incorruptible character, he
is not guileless. For this reason he doubts Domiciano de la Gándara's
sincerity when the latter pledges himself to the revolutionary cause.
Filomeno tells the Colonel that he can travel under escort to the
rebels' headquarters, but safeguards his own position in case Domiciano
should turn out to be a spy: "Los cincuenta bolívares," he observes,
"te serán entregados al pisar las líneas revolucionarias. Irás sin armas,
y el guía lleva la orden de tronarte si le infundes la menor sospecha"
(756).

In this novel the opposing forces of tyranny and liberty are not
given equal emphasis. Valle-Inclán is far more concerned with the
implications of oppression, as is fitting in a subcontinent much more
familiar with it than with freedom. Consequently Tirano Banderas

dominates the novel while Filomeno Cuevas occupies a subordinate position, despite the fact that he acts as a catalyst, causing the downfall and death of Tierra Caliente's strong man.

b) *Sánchez Ocaña*

Unlike Filomeno Cuevas, Sánchez Ocaña is a professional politician and public orator. Therefore he is not spared Valle-Inclán's merciless satire. He appears in two episodes only and emerges as a man of no substance. Valle-Inclán probably visualised him as the end product of nineteenth-century liberal democracy, a form of government for which, like other Spanish writers of the same period, he had nothing but scorn.

Sánchez Ocaña is first seen when he gives a speech at the Circo Harris. The author notes his use of all the tricks of the politician's trade: "El orador desleía el boladillo en el vaso de agua. Cataba un sorbo: hacía engalle: se tiraba de los almidonados puños . . ." (702). Later in the same scene, Valle-Inclán compares him to an opera-singer, stressing, as is his habit, the essential artificiality of a character who is acting a part: "El orador sacaba los puños, lucía las mancuernas, se acercaba a las luces del proscenio. Le acogió una salva de aplausos. Con saludo de tenor remontóse en su aria . . ." (703).

In his portrayal of Filomeno Cuevas, Valle-Inclán is at pains to establish that he is a man of action rather than of words. The reverse applies to Doctor Alfredo Sánchez Ocaña, a past master of the clichés of political rhetoric. Such effect as he has is on the ear alone, something which Nachito inadvertently makes clear when he remarks: " ¡Sabe, amigo, que habla muy lindo el Doctor Sánchez Ocaña!" (755).

c) *Roque Cepeda*

Roque Cepeda is the most complex and unusual character in *Tirano Banderas,* although not necessarily the most convincing. He belongs to that small band of enlightened characters who do not suffer the degradation implicit in the *esperpento* aesthetic. Since

Valle stated that he had Francisco Madero in mind when fashioning this character, it is worth examining Madero's career to see what similarities there are between the two men.

Francisco Madero, born in 1873, was a rather unlikely figure in the Mexico of his period, in that he was an idealistic and humanitarian man who did not lust after power for its own sake. He was the son of wealthy landowners and was converted to spiritualism during a visit to France. This affected his outlook towards his fellow-men. He wrote: "Spiritualism invites a more elevated conception of Divinity, and an admission of the immutability of divine law; as a consequence [it also invites] a recognition that the sufferings of humanity are caused by its own imperfections and are not the result of divine ire."[34] After Porfirio Díaz was forced into exile in 1911, Madero took over the presidency. Díaz is said to have remarked at this juncture: "Madero has unleashed a tiger; let us see if he can control him." These proved to be prophetic words as Madero was assassinated in 1913 after a coup by Huerta had caused the downfall of his government.

The points of contact between Madero and Roque Cepeda are clear but of a general nature only. Both are educated creoles devoid of material ambitions who share a mystical bent.

Don Roque appears to live on a different plane from that of the other characters. This is because of his mystical inclinations. Into him Valle has poured his preoccupation with the occult and with esoteric doctrines such as Gnosticism: "Don Roque era varón de muy varias y desconcertantes lecturas, que por el sendero teosófico lindaban con la cábala, el ocultismo y la filosofía alejandrina" (781). Predictably, granted the author's interest in the Gnostics' understanding of time, Roque Cepeda sees man as a criminal condemned to endure temporality in order to expiate his sins: "Para Don Roque

---

[34]See Charles Curtis Cumberland, *Mexican Revolution: Genesis under Madero* (Austin, 1952), 33.

los hombres eran ángeles desterrados: Reos de un crimen celeste, indultaban su culpa teologal por los caminos del tiempo, que son los caminos del mundo" (780).

For this strange revolutionary, political activity and religious feeling cannot be divorced, since both are manifestations of how we comprehend eternity: "La intuición de eternidad trascendida es la conciencia religiosa. Y en nuestro ideario, la piedra angular, la redención del indio, es un sentimiento fundamentalmente cristiano" (780). Valle-Inclán often likens Roque Cepeda to a saint but, as in the case of Filomeno Cuevas, goodness does not signify naiveté. His understanding of more devious minds is shown by his reaction to Tirano Banderas' overtures of peace and promise of fair play in the next elections. When the Tyrant expresses his willingness to declare a truce and free the political prisoners, Cepeda's misgivings are strong enough to be betrayed by his facial expression: "Don Roque le miraba con honrada y apacible expresión, tan ingenua que descubría las sospechas del ánimo: — ¡Una tregua! —" (814).

If Filomeno Cuevas represents the man of action and Sánchez Ocaña the manipulator of outdated words, Roque Cepeda is the man who combines originality of thought with concrete political activity. The fusion of meditation and action stems from his belief that religious or philosophic convictions are inseparable from political activity. Within the body of Valle-Inclán's production, Roque Cepeda is unique as an example of the politically orientated mystic. The nearest approaches to this character are Michael Bakunin in *Baza de espadas* (1932) and a fellow-Anarchist, Fermín Salvochea, in the unfinished novel *El trueno dorado* (1936).

The Gachupín

a) *Baron Benicarlés*

From the *Sonatas* onwards, Valle was well-nigh obsessed by the feeling that the times were out of joint for his country; that the strong had given way to the weak and degenerate, and that cruelty and ruthlessness no longer had the justification of ardent religious conviction. Since Valle barely ever acts as the omnipotent author, the reader is required to pick up hints and to form his own conclusions about the characters and the subject-matter with which he is presented.

In the context of *Tirano Banderas,* it cannot be without significance that the representative of the Spanish Crown in Tierra Caliente is a foppish homosexual and a drug-addict to boot. In addition, when Valle introduces this character he avails himself of a device which is also used in the *Ruedo ibérico* novels to satirize members of the aristocracy. This consists of a bald list of their innumerable titles. The contrast thus created between the effete or degenerate nobleman and his magnificent string of titles reflects the absurdity inherent in the world of the *esperpento.* However, it is a fact that *Tirano Banderas* contains far more characters who either completely elude the scornful treatment of the author/demigod or are found to have redeeming features. The Barón de Benicarlés is in the latter category and is not always treated as a figure of fun. Instead, his rather pathetic figure arouses the same feelings of sorrow as Pascual Friolera in *Los cuernos de don Friolera.*

Benicarlés is not without sensitivity, and he notes sadly at one point that the Spanish Minister is not asked to participate in the conspiracies organised by the representatives of more important countries: "Los tres diplomáticos, el yanqui, el alemán, el austríaco, ensayando el terceto de su mutua discrepancia, poníanle sobre los hilos una intriga, y experimentaba un dolor sincero, reconociendo que en aquel mundo, su mundo, todas las cábalas se hacían sin contar con el Ministro de España" (808). The word from this quotation which is worth underlining in a world of poor actors and automata is 'sincero'.

Evidently the Tyrant finds Benicarlés' fondness for bullfighters politically useful if personally repugnant: proof of homosexual

practices is useful to force the Spanish Minister to toe the line.
But Benicarlés, schooled in deviousness, knows how to counter such
moves by bribing the Tyrant's stupid emissary, Don Celes Galindo.

The languid transvestite, with his morphine-glazed eyes, his lap-
dog and vulgar male lover, causes the spirit of a sensual vicereine of
earlier times to weep bitter tears. Here Spain's past, healthy and
vigorous despite its excesses of cruelty, is contrasted with the
esperpento of the present: "La sombra de la ardiente virreina,
refugiada en el fondo del jardín, mirando la fiesta de amor sin mujeres,
lloró muchas veces, incomprensiva, celosa, tapándose la cara" (684).

Thus the Baron is primarily a symbol of Spain's decadence and
loss of status in the world. Valle-Inclán also uses this character to
jeer at his own earlier manner. In the *Sonata de otoño,* Bradomín
asks Concha if he can act as her handmaiden (II, 128); in *Tirano
Banderas,* the Baron's lover, Currito mi Alma, uses almost the same
words when asking Benicarlés if he can assist him as he dresses (797).

b) *Don Celestino Galindo*

Don Celes is the least positive character among the prominent
gachupines. A fool, a bumbler and a bully, he is also a prosperous
businessman whose chief aim is to safeguard his own position in the
country by remaining in Santos Banderas' good graces. Don Celes is
used by the Tyrant in an attempt to ensure Benicarlés' good behaviour.
But this attempt at moral blackmail fails because the Baron is
conscious of Don Celes' stupidity and proceeds to bribe him with
prospects of a ministerial post in Spain. Don Celes examines the idea
with relish, betraying that shallow form of patriotic fervour so
common among Valle's characters of this period: "Emilio [Castelar]
le llamaría por cable . . . ¡Todo por mi Patria! " (799). But finally
cupidity defeats political ambition because a worrying thought enters
his head obliging him to cry off: "El ilustre gachupín temía la
mengua de sus lucros si trocaba la explotación de cholos y morenos
por el servicio de la Madre Patria" (799).

The astute Tyrant is conscious that Celestino is a very materialistic man, and it is an appeal to his greed which turns the *gachupín* into his ally. Santos Banderas reminds Don Celes that a political coup would jeopardise the position of Tierra Caliente's landowners: "La revolución representa la ruina de los estancieros españoles" (681). The Tyrant hopes that by making it clear to the Spanish residents that they would be at a loss without him, he will find it easier to raise a large loan from them.

In the case of Don Celes as with all the other *gachupines,* be they major or subsidiary characters, the characteristic Valle chooses to highlight is venality. Inevitably this shortcoming goes hand in hand with selfishness and total indifference to others.

c) *Quintín Pereda*

Valle-Inclán usually refers to the Spanish pawnbroker with cutting irony as "el honrado gachupín". This is one of the short, descriptive phrases attached to different characters in the later novels which are the *esperpento*'s answer to epic epithets. "Peredita", as he is sometimes called,[35] is one of the most malevolent characters in this novel and, as I have already mentioned, he receives his just deserts at the hands of Zacarías el Cruzado. But caution should be exercised when considering Valle's attitude to this character since Pereda has been deliberately overdrawn to serve a dual purpose. Valle uses him both to state a few home truths about the grasping *gachupines* and also to satirise the popular conception of the miser "grinding the faces of the poor". If Valle were not intent on parodying a cliché of popular nineteenth-century literature, the two poor whites treated so harshly by the pawnbroker would have been sympathetically portrayed. The individuals in question are a blind pianist and his frail daughter who

[35]Valle avails himself of the Mexican's fondness for diminutives when satirising various characters. Thus the dreaded Tyrant becomes "el Generalito"; the miserly pawnbroker, "Peredita"; and, with a rather different end in view, Currito mi Alma addresses Benicarlés as "Isabelita".

eke out their living as street entertainers. Dehumanising metaphors
are applied to the father, and the daughter is a shadowy, unattractive
creature. Yet Pereda's refusal to give them a further fortnight to meet
the interest due on the piano gives Valle the opportunity to comment
on the grasping nature of a typical *gachupín*. The daughter pleads
with the pawnbroker to exercise charity and, having failed, adds
bitterly: "No sea usted de su tierra Señor Peredita" (739). This
remark infuriates the pawnbroker who retorts that if it were not for
the Spaniards they would still be walking about in feathers.

Pereda's miserliness is not confined to those he considers his
inferiors. When Don Celes gives his grandchildren some of the
traditional bells sold during the religious festivals, Quintín suspects
at once that there is a motive behind this gesture. Don Celes takes
the opportunity to tell Melcíades, Pereda's son, that he would like his
father to attend an extraordinary meeting at the Casino. Don
Quintín's wrath knows no bounds:

> Me nombrarán de alguna comisión, tendré que abandonar por ratos
> el establecimiento, posiblemente me veré incluido para contribuir...
> De tales reuniones siempre sale una lista de suscripciones. El
> Casino está pervirtiendo su funcionamiento y el objetivo de sus
> estatutos. De centro recreativo se ha vuelto un sacadineros (742).

All the *gachupines* without exception are seen to be motivated
only by the grossest self-interest. The author also condemns them
because of their ingrained superiority complex and insulting treatment of Indians and half-castes. Thus within the scope of *Tirano
Banderas* the *gachupín* is an outright villain. Such a comment
would be irrelevant if one were considering, say, the *Ruedo ibérico*
cycle, for the characters in these novels are almost to a man despicable
puppets. But one way in which *Tirano Banderas* differs from Valle-
Inclán's other works of the twenties is that there is a more equal
distribution between the forces of good and evil. Hence the
significance of the author's denigration of all the Spaniards involved.

VII

Narrative Technique

The novels of Valle-Inclán's maturity contain certain features
which are the result of the author's clear-cut views on the novel. The
most important of these features are:— 1. A pronounced stress on
dialogue; 2. An indifference to analysis of character or psychological
studies which, to some extent, is a corollary of the first; 3. The
portrayal of an entire community rather than one of its segments;
4. An evident desire to achieve an overall effect of synthesis which is
accompanied by intense stylisation of character and background. I
shall consider each of these points in turn.

Valle gave a lucid and detailed explanation for the stress on
dialogue in his works during an interview in 1926 with José Montero
Alonso. In the course of the conversation, Valle described dialogue
as the best method for achieving the impassivity required by the
esperpento aesthetic:

> Escribo casi siempre en forma escénica, dialogada . . . Escribo de
> esa manera porque me gusta mucho, porque me parece que es la
> forma literaria mejor, más serena y más 'impasible' de conducir la
> acción. Amo la impasibilidad en el arte. Quiero que mis personajes
> se presenten siempre solos y sean en todo momento ellos, sin el
> comentario, sin la explicación de su creador. Que todo lo sea, en
> fin, la acción misma. En este aspecto existen dos formas literarias:
> ésta, cuyo interés reside en los mismos personajes desde el momento
> en que se presentan, y la que, cuando los personajes y la acción
> son triviales, hace poner al autor el comentario y la justificación
> de lo que pasa. En este caso, pone el escritor lo que no hay en los
> hechos, recargando la obra, incluyéndose en ella como un nuevo
> personaje . . . Del primer tipo de arte — arte 'impasible,' . . . hay
> un ejemplo en Shakespeare. Del segundo, en Anatole France y en
> Proust. A mí, de esas dos formas, la que me gusta es la primera.[36]

[36]*La novela de hoy,* 15 November 1929.

In 1928, speaking on this occasion to Gregorio Martínez Sierra, Valle returned to the same question. Referring to his projected *Ruedo ibérico* cycle, he stated: " . . . busco más que el fabular novelesco, la sátira encubierta bajo ficciones casi de teatro. Digo casi de teatro porque todo está expresado por medio de diálogos, y el sentir mío me guardo de expresarlo directamente".[37]

The dramatic bias of Valle's later novels by its very nature excludes analysis of character. This is made clear in the first of the two extracts quoted above by Valle's allusion to Proust as an author whose approach to the novel held no appeal for him. The point is also borne out by the presentation of the characters in *Tirano Banderas*: only in a very few cases are we given details about their background and thought processes. Such information as is given tends to be rather sparse. We learn that Santos Banderas picked up the habit of chewing coca leaves whilst on a military campaign in Peru; that Benicarlés can still recall a scandal centred on him "en una Corte de Europa" (798), and that Zacarías was once a bandit (757). Benicarlés emerges as a partial exception in another way for, after he has given himself a shot of morphine, the author uses the stream of consciousness technique to describe the disconnected thoughts surging through his mind as he is conveyed to the British Legation. However, in general terms, *Tirano Banderas* conforms to the views expressed by Valle-Inclán.

If one examines the composition of Valle's later novels, it becomes obvious that he had rejected the more traditional type in which the interest is focused throughout on a small cluster of characters, in favour of one concerned with a cross-section of society. Consequently *Tirano Banderas* and the *Ruedo ibérico* novels contain a veritable swarm of characters. Many of these are given no prominence whatsoever, owing to the author's view that once a character had served

[37]*ABC*, 7 December 1928.

his purpose he should be discarded for good. Valle's concentration on the community as a whole, as opposed to a segment of it, is related to his views on contemporary history:

> . . . la vida marcha ahora por la ruta de lo social — y esta interpretación se refleja lógica y necesariamente en la novela que es la historia. En *La Guerra y la Paz,* Tolstoi vio ya esta supremacía de la masa.[38]

Whilst theoretically *Tirano Banderas* is concerned with a community and not an individual, in practice the Tyrant cannot be dissociated from the country and its inhabitants. It is true that he figures only in certain sections of the novel, yet Emma Speratti has rightly pointed out that Santos Banderas acts as the novel's pivot: ". . . Tirano Banderas es el eje de este mundo sombrío, fuerza implacable desencadenada por un mecanismo de situaciones y acontecimientos y capaz de desencadenar otros cuyo fin no es completamente claro, ni quiere serlo, en el libro".[39]

Thus this novel simultaneously confirms and contradicts Valle's views. It confirms them because he is concerned with the fate of a country, Tierra Caliente, but is at odds with them because Santos Banderas is very much a central character. It is precisely the ominous presence of the tyrant which gives this work an impression of unity lacking in, say, *Viva mi dueño,* despite the fact that the underlying structure of the second is just as formal as that of *Tirano Banderas* itself.

In a country where cacti, swamps, plains, llamas, guanacos and jungle commingle quite happily, where Mexican words such as *chamaco, chingado, hipil* and *metate* jostle with terms peculiar to other parts of Latin America, and where the protagonist, according to the author's own words, is modelled on a number of the continent's

---

[38]Quoted by José Balseiro in *Cuatro individualistas de España* (Chapel Hill, 1949), 170.
[39]*La elaboración artística en Tirano Banderas,* 126.

tyrants, it is suitable to speak in terms of synthesis. This aspect of
Tirano Banderas has not been ignored by students of Valle-Inclán's
works. It is given clear expression in an article by David Lagmanovich:

> Puede concluirse que es Méjico que está indicado, aunque queda
> mucho sin explicación. En cuanto al aspecto físico del paisaje, lo
> que da su característica es la multiplicidad de rasgos distintos . . .
> El paisaje es irreal y compuesto . . . la visión de Valle-Inclán busca
> constantemente la integración, no la particularización. Y esa
> integración se logra mediante el aporte amplísimo de vocablos y
> factores, y mediante la técnica de la juxtaposición, muchas veces
> violenta, muchas veces arbitraria. Se obtiene así una especie de
> rapsodia americana que, en último término, es irreductible al
> análisis minucioso, pues su valor principal consiste precisamente
> en la idea predominante, y a cada paso realizada, de la síntesis. [40]

The fact that synthesis is so obvious a feature of Valle-Inclán's
mature production has caused critics in the last few years to link
him with the Expressionists. Juan Guerrero Zamora, who has written
an excellent analysis of Valle-Inclán's plays in his vast *Historia del
teatro contemporáneo,* considers the rôle of synthesis in Expressionist
drama, and concludes that it is the key to the whole: "Esto es el
expresionismo. Una síntesis. Una sugerencia expresiva indicando el
fondo del problema".[41]

It would be foolhardy to label Valle-Inclán an Expressionist,
since in his later years he did not adhere to any one movement in the
arts. At the same time he was well aware of new literary and artistic
movements, being particularly sensitive to developments in painting.
This was due, no doubt, to his very plastic conception of literature. It
is a fact that if one considers the manifestations of Expressionism in
literature, painting and the film, a number of similarities are revealed
between these works and the production of Valle's maturity.

In any definition of Expressionism, be it concerned with the
visual arts or with literature, certain key words recur. They are

[40]"La visión de América en *Tirano Banderas*", 268-9.
[41]*Historia del teatro contemporáneo,* Vol. II, 60.

distortion, exaggeration and caricature. The German theorist of Expressionism, Kasimir Edschmid, stated that the Expressionists were in revolt against the attitude to the arts manifested by their immediate predecessors, that is, the Impressionists and the Naturalists. They were not concerned with reproducing the outward appearance of an object, preferring, instead, to capture its essence or idea:

> L'artiste expressioniste, non pas réceptif mais véritablement créateur, cherche, au lieu d'un effet momentané, la signification éternelle des faits et des objets. Il faut, disent les expressionistes, se détacher de la nature et s'efforcer de dégager l'expression la plus expressive d'un objet.[42]

These tenets led to an art characterized by the following features: the artist's vision of the world was extremely subjective; abstract localities were preferred to realistic ones; objects were personified; types rather than individuals were employed; the artist sought to fire his audience with moral indignation; and, finally, Expressionists viewed nature as fundamentally hostile. The following description of the film sets for *The Cabinet of Doctor Caligari* (1919), which were created by three Expressionist painters, brings out the intensity of stylisation favoured by these artists:

> . . . its sets transform material objects into emotional ornaments: jagged angles, oblique chimneys, crazy rooftops, zigzag perspectives, painted shadows illogically matched with the lighting effects —all form a nightmarish approximation to houses, walls, corridors and landscapes.[43]

Through a detailed examination of the imagery used by Valle-Inclán in *Tirano Banderas,* further similarities between Expressionism and Valle's own art can be revealed. However, it should be emphasized that the art of Valle-Inclán in the twenties is itself a synthesis, showing affinities with more than one contemporary movement in the spheres of painting and literature. Indeed in *Tirano Banderas* there is no

---

[42]Quoted by Lotte H. Eisner in *L'Ecran démoniaque* (Paris, 1952), 28.
[43]"The *Sunday Times* Guide to the Modern Movement in the Arts", 18 June, 1967.

allusion to Expressionism, whilst on two occasions the author refers to Cubism.[44]

[44]See pp. 705 & 787.

VIII

Stylistic Features

a) *Dehumanisation*

It is not my intention to trace the development of Valle's use of various forms of dehumanisation from their tentative beginnings in his very earliest short stories. This is an aspect of his work already considered in detail and at some length by other critics. For our present purposes it suffices to say that even a cursory reading of *Tirano Banderas* reveals that the vast majority of the characters are subjected to various forms of dehumanisation congruous with the god-like posture Valle assumes towards them.

Because Valle-Inclán's mature production pullulates with these grotesque images, it is convenient to divide them into categories. The types of dehumanisation most favoured by the author are those involving characters viewed as animals and as puppets or dolls. Often a particular image accompanies a character throughout a work: one aspect of his appearance or nature is singled out and he is type-cast by the description repeatedly applied to him. This may arise even in the case of minor characters who figure in one episode only. In such cases it may appear that the device is being handled mechanically and unimaginatively, but it should be recalled that the insistent use of one dehumanising image reflects the author's scorn of his sub-human characters who are in this way deprived of any complexity of spirit. In his use of dehumanising techniques Valle, like the Expressionists, is stylising an object so as to accentuate its latent physiognomy.

1. *Animals*

Tirano Banderas, like the *Ruedo ibérico* cycle, is peopled by a weird fauna of large mammals, birds and rodents. Needless to say, few of the animal metaphors reflect well on the characters to whom

they are applied. Santos Banderas is often qualified as a sacred crow
or an owl. He is also described as a rat, owing to his suspicious nature,
which makes him appear as though he is sniffing about him for
trouble or conspiracies in the making:

> Tirano Banderas, con paso de rata fisgona, . . . abandonó el juego
> de la rana (692).

> Tirano Banderas, con olisca de rata fisgona, abandonó la rueda de
> lisonjeros compadres . . . (705)

> Sin alterar su paso de rata fisgona, salió a la recámara donde se
> recluía la hija (830).

A subsidiary character who always has the same animal metaphor
applied to him is Velones, the blind man, who is consistently described
as "el ciego lechuzo". In the case of Niño Santos the owl is used to
suggest the bird of prey, but when it is applied to Velones it must
refer either to his blindness or to his physical appearance. Since the
blind man's piano is also described as a "piano lechuzo" (717), it is
obvious that from the author's viewpoint there is nothing to
distinguish the man from the object.

There is less desire to qualify a character precisely when he is
only playing a bit-part. Tirano Banderas' assistants are described as
"dos lagartijos con brillantes uniformes" (788); a group of *gachupines,*
uneasy in the presence of the Tyrant, shift their position "como
ganado inquieto por la mosca" (679); one of the Tyrant's henchmen
has teeth reminiscent of a wolf: "El retinto garabato del bigote,
dábale fiero resalte al arregaño lobatón de los dientes . . ." (677).

The *gachupines* may be 'mineralised' as well as animalised. The
section within the novel which is devoted to them is entitled 'Cuarzos
ibéricos' and one of their number, the landowner Teodosio del Araco,
is described as an "íbero granítico" (696). Oddly, the most malevolent
gachupín, Quintín Pereda, is never directly described as an animal.
But at one point, Valle notes that there is nothing to distinguish him
from his cat, either in physical appearance or in their reaction to a
particular occurrence:

El empeñista acariciaba su gato, un maltés vejete y rubiales, que trascendía el absurdo de parecerse a su dueño. El gato y el empeñista miraron a la puerta, desdoblando el mismo gesto de alarma (764).

It is worth noting that according to the author, it is absurd for the cat to resemble his master rather than vice-versa.

2. *Puppets and dolls*

A rich variety of puppet metaphors is applied to the subsidiary characters. They include *autómatas alemanes* (790), *muñeco automático* (817) and *bailarín de alambre* (793).   Related to these are images equating characters with statues or figurines, normally of idols.   Domiciano de la Gándara has a "vientre rotundo de ídolo tibetano" (675), variations on this description being employed whenever he is introduced.   Thus, like Don Celes, this character is typecast by his paunch, something which deprives him of any spirituality.

The Tyrant's stiffness is accentuated through being likened to a wooden effigy.   This stiffness refers as much to his love of punctilio as to his inflexible moral code:

El Tirano se inclinó con aquel ademán mesurado y rígido de figura de palo (710).

Al cabo, resolviéndose, hizo una cortesía de estantigua, y comenzó a subir la escalera (714).

The final degradation Valle inflicts on his characters is to describe them as shadows or vague shapes:

Eran sobre el hueco profundo de sombra, oscuros bultos de borroso realce (714).

Por un terradillo blanco de luna, dos sombras fugitivas arrastran un piano negro (827).

Raro prestigio cobró de pronto aquella sombra, y aquella voz de caña hueca, raro imperio (692).

Evidently in these cases symbolism is linked with an artistic effect, since Valle is always creating word paintings.   The same fusion is to be found in his use of light effects, a further stylistic feature to be studied in this chapter.

3. *The Metamorphosis of Objects*

In the topsy-turvy world of the *esperpento* it is not only the human elements which suffer transmutation. Objects too may be humanised or, so to speak, transposed to another key. In his later works, Valle uses this technique consistently, although not as frequently as that of dehumanisation, since he is more concerned with the absurdity of human beings. His aim is to confuse animal, vegetable and mineral life in one great, meaningless jumble. Thus a small folding table becomes a spider:

> Niño Santos . . . le indicó la mesilla de campamento que, en el vano de un arco, abría sus compases de araña (679).

A light carriage has the false air of a fop:

> Por la conga del convento, saltarín y liviano, con morisquetas de lechugino, rodaba el quitrí de Don Celes (683).

Buildings, like characters, may be qualified by a theatrical image:

> El fuerte de Santa Mónica descollaba el dramón de su arquitectura en el luminoso ribazo marino (792).

Alternatively, they may be switched to the animal kingdom:

> Los muros de reductos y hornabaques destacaban su ruda geometría castrense, como buldogs trascendidos a expresión matemática (791).

The vegetable and mineral kingdoms may be fused as in the following concise image:

> Miró su reloj, una cebolla de plata, y le dio cuerda con dos llaves . . . (708).

A human being may strike a jarring note amid the harmony and repose of objects:

> Desasistido de emoción, árido, tímido, como si no tuviese dinero, penetró en el estrado vacío, turbando la dorada simetría de espejos y consolas (685).

and the world of phenomena may ape the ridiculous behaviour of mankind:

> Y la luna, puesta la venda de una nube, juega con las estrellas a la gallina ciega, sobre la revolucionada Santa Fe de Tierra Firme (827).

All these images serve to underscore Valle's view that the world is grotesque and amorphous. Within it, the most despicable and puny element is man himself.

b) *Theatrical analogies*

The theatrical analogies employed by Valle-Inclán serve a dual purpose: to accentuate the novel's similarity to a play in terms of its organization and, secondly, to drive home the artificiality of the characters' gestures and attitudes. Many of the images employed do not refer to the formal theatre but embrace other entertainments such as the circus, opera and melodrama. Terms such as guignol and melodrama are included because they harmonise with the *esperpento* spirit.

Of particular importance in *Tirano Banderas* is grand guignol. Apart from isolated instances of its use in the novel, 'book' III of 'Noche de farra' is called 'Guiñol dramático'. This book describes the arrival of the police at Cucarachita's brothel in search of Domiciano de la Gándara who is able to escape just in time. As he leaves the brothel he sees the police arriving to detain him: " ¡Fue como truco de melodrama! " the author exclaims, thus setting the tone for the entire episode. The 'book' resembles guignol owing to its frenetic pace, melodramatic moments and to the part played in it by Mayor Abilio del Valle. He stalks about the brothel cleaving the air with his sword and issuing dire threats to the *madame* should she be lying about Domiciano's whereabouts.

Apart from guignol, which is a very suitable term to employ in the context of *Tirano Banderas,* the novel is characterised by a singular variety of theatrical images. Some of them are intended to underline a deliberate piece of play-acting or affectation on the part of a character, whilst others illustrate the author's attitude to his creations. There are some characters to whom a good many of these images are applied, but others —the Tyrant is one such— are barely ever equated with actors. Santos Banderas tends to react with irritation when he feels a person's behaviour is affected. This is brought out very clearly in the interview he grants to Doña Rosita Pintado who has come to plead on behalf of her son, Marco Aurelio:

Doña Rosita Pintado, caído el rebozo, con dramática escuela, se arrojó a las plantas del Tirano:
—¡Generalito, no es justicia lo que se hace con mi chamaco!
Avinagró el gesto la momia indiana:
—Alce doña Rosita; no es un tablado de comedia la audiencia del Primer Magistrado de la Nación (790).

Doña Rosita is by no means the only character guilty of indulging in cheap, stagey gestures:

Doña Lupita jugó el rebocillo como una dama de teatro (691).

Saludó [el Doctor Polaco] con una curvatura pomposa y escenográfica, colocándose la chistera bajo el brazo (823).

El Licenciado Sánchez Ocaña, un poco pálido, con afectación teatral, sonreía removiendo la cucharilla en el vaso de agua (702).

The *gachupín*, Celestino Galindo, who is never equated with an animal, is visualised instead as a nervous actor:

Don Celes,. . . poco a poco, iba inflando la botarga, pero con una sombra de recelo, una íntima y remota cobardía de cómico silbado (680).

. . . tenía esa actitud petulante y preocupada del cómico que entre bastidores espera su salida a escena (708).

Valle-Inclán also avails himself of a theatrical parallel to describe in acid terms Don Celes' particular brand of patriotic feeling:

¡Todo por mi Patria! Aquella matrona entrada en carnes, corona, rodela y estoque, le conmovía como dama de tablas que corta el verso en la tramoya de candilejas, bambalinas y telones (799).

Evidently, one of the most artificial characters involved is the effeminate Barón de Benicarlés. Valle is apt to apply a mask image to highlight the grotesque effect created by his heavy make-up:

El Ministro de su Majestad Católica sonreía, y sobre la crasa rasura, el colorete abriéndose en grietas tenía un sarcasmo de careta chafada (800).

Merlín, el gozque faldero, le lamía el colorete y adobaba el mascarón esparciéndole el afeite con la espátula linguaria (795). In the case of Santos Banderas and Zacarías, the mask image does not carry the same connotations, for it is always qualified as a "máscara indiana". Its sole purpose is to indicate the impassivity of the Indian who seldom betrays emotion through facial expression.

Closely connected with the term mask is *mueca*. Nearly every description of the Tyrant is accompanied by an allusion to his grimace and there are times when the entire man is reduced to a grimace. It is often described as a 'mueca verde' owing to the green spittle trickling from the corners of his mouth:

Tirano Banderas, rasgada la boca por la verde mueca, se volvió al coro de comparsas . . . (711)

La mueca verde remegía los venenos de una befa aun soturna y larvada en los repliegues del ánimo (810).

La momia acogió con una mueca enigmática . . . (680)

Pausado y prolijo, rumiando la coca, hacía sus tiradas, y en los yerros su boca rasgábase toda verde, como una mueca . . . (689)

Many of the other characters, with the understandable exception of the few virtuous ones, bear this characteristic stamp of the *esperpento*. However it is only applied consistently to the Tyrant because he is more dehumanised than anybody else.

In *Tirano Banderas* the frequent allusions to entertainments and actors have the additional value of harmonising with the carnival atmosphere of the background. The symbolism is complicated by the fact that the celebrations are associated with the dead. This is why *mueca* is the most fitting symbol for the novel: it brings to mind the fixed grimace of a corpse and also explains why the term should be consistently applied to Tirano Banderas himself. Valle makes it clear through associated terms such as *momia* and *calavera* that Niño Santos experiences only a death in life.

c) *Cinematographic techniques*

The similarity between some of the techniques employed by Valle-

Inclán in his later novels and those of the cinema has been considered in the past. José Balseiro is among those who have called attention to the influence of the cinema in *Tirano Banderas*. In his view:

> . . . tiene de la película la esquematización de la materia y el elemento plástico acelerado mediante efectiva desintegración: justo sentido del elemento esencial y la poliédrica visualización de las ideas, junto a superposiciones de planos, los primeros términos a manera de close-ups, y la sugestión de motivos más que la realización cabal de las escenas.[45]

Antonio Risco, after some consideration of the subject, concludes that the affinity is spurious because, he argues, there is no "continuidad de sentido que ligue planos y secuencias". Instead Valle's art resembles that of a painter and is concerned primarily with space. He concludes:

> Valle se interesa mucho más por la eficacia inmediata de cada escena en sí misma que por narrar una historia. A veces casi parece hacer abstracción del pasado y del futuro para convertir la obra en una simple sucesión de presentes.[46]

It should be pointed out that Risco is concerned exclusively with the *Ruedo ibérico* novels, and these are longer and more fragmentary than *Tirano Banderas*. They also contain many more characters than this novel. Thus it is easier to justify this argument if one omits *Tirano Banderas* which is given more unity by the presence of a central character. This does not mean that *Tirano Banderas* is a cinematic rather than a pictorial novel. It is both, since the two terms are not mutually exclusive. For example, some of the films of Michelangelo Antonioni, such as *L'Avventura* (1959) and *Il Deserto Rosso* (1963), consist of carefully composed images and are virtually plotless. What this director seeks to convey is a mood and an impression of character through a series of very slow-moving scenes.

What has tended to happen in the course of this century is that

[45] *Cuatro individualistas de España*, 164.

[46] *La estética de Valle-Inclán*, 128 & 131.

both the film director and the novelist have become progressively more critical of the conventions governing their particular art form. This has brought the two genres closer together, with the result that a film director can, quite literally, make 'pictures', and a novelist like Valle-Inclán abandon the rôle of story-teller or psychologist in favour of techniques traditionally associated with the theatre or the cinema.

José Balseiro limits himself to general points of contact between *Tirano Banderas* and the cinema, but it is also possible to point out instances where the author avails himself of specific cinematographic techniques. These include: abrupt switches of scene, like camera-cuts from one shot to the next; close-ups of characters' faces or other details of their person; and angled shots in which a scene is described from the viewpoint of one individual, sometimes providing a very strange angle of vision.

Abrupt cuts may be used to impress upon the reader that some of the events taking place in different localities are occurring simultaneously. This is most obvious in an episode I have already mentioned in a different context, namely, 'Guiñol dramático'. Here Valle uses the common cinematic device of parallel action, cutting from the plight of the pursued to the angry pursuer hot on their heels. Thus 'scene' or subdivision II of this chapter describes Domiciano and Nachito taking refuge in the bedroom of the student Marco Aurelio. This scene ends with Domiciano leaping out of the window while Nachito, lacking the courage to follow him, exclaims in bemused fashion: " ¡Hay que ser gato! " (728). This is followed by an abrupt cut back to Cucarachita's brothel where the irate Mayor del Valle is seeking to discover Domiciano's whereabouts. This occupies scene III in its entirety. Scene IV starts with the following words: "Y Nachito Veguillas aún exprime su gesto turulato frente a la ventana del estudiante." (729). In other words, there has been no lapse of time between scenes II and IV, and the major is striding about the bordello at precisely the same moment as Nachito is standing at the window.

There are also occasions when Valle views a scene from a rather strange angle. The most interesting application of this technique is to be found in a description of the Tyrant as he is being shaved by his barber. The room and its occupants are described as Niño Santos sees them reflected in his shaving mirror:

> El Mayor se inmovilizaba en el saludo militar. Niño Santos, mirando de refilón el espejillo que tenía delante, veía proyectarse la puerta y una parte de la estancia con perspectiva desconcertada . . . (789).

Another instance of this technique involves a general description of Santa Fe at night. It turns out that the scene is being viewed by the Tyrant through a telescope from the vantage-point of the monastery he inhabits. The last words of the description provide the link between the scene and the man viewing it: "A lo lejos . . . calcaba el negro perfil de su arquitectura San Martín de los Mostenses" (819). This marks the end of a book. The next chapter, 'Paso de bufones', starts as follows: "Tirano Banderas, en la ventana, apuntaba su catalejo sobre la ciudad de Santa Fe . . ." (819). The beginning of the first book, 'Icono del tirano', is also described from the dictator's angle of vision. Here the camera appears to be gradually moving in and narrowing down the field of vision until the Tyrant himself appears in close-up. Following a succinct description of the geographical location of Santa Fe, Valle introduces the monastery which is to become a constant feature of the background. Then attention is focused on the Tyrant himself. There is a further laconic description —on this occasion a brief biography of Niño Santos— after which the actions taking place in the monastery grounds are viewed from his position at a window. Furthermore, the reader is reminded that the actions are being viewed from this vantage point by allusions to the dictator's presence there and, at the start of the fifth scene, to his retiring into the room (677).

Also reminiscent of a film is Valle's custom of fastening attention on some small detail. This may be done to obtain a humorous or artistic effect or, alternatively, to disconcert the reader, as in the following example in which the detail is the eye of a horse:

> El Cruzado miraba por los hierros la figura toda en sombra. El ojo enorme del caballo recibía por veces una luz en el juego de las siluetas que accionaban cortando el círculo del candil (769).

The next example describes the discomfiture of the *gachupines* in the presence of Niño Santos. Here their state of mind is rendered accurately through the minute observation of a series of nervous gestures:

> Se descompuso la ringla de gachupines. Los charolados pies juanetudos cambiaron de loseta. Las manos, enguantadas y torponas, se removieron indecisas sin saber dónde posarse. En un tácito acuerdo, los gachupines jugaron con las brasileñas leontinas de sus relojes (678).

This is a much more subtle and successful way of pinpointing their embarrassment than by making a bald statement to this effect, something which would in any event run contrary to the impassivity implicit in the *esperpento*. By indicating that they are all doing the same thing simultaneously, the description has the additional advantage of bringing out the *gachupines'* resemblance to a chorus in a play.

It would prove both worthwhile and relatively simple to turn this novel into a film-script. The only real difficulty would be presented by the cultivated artificiality of the background, for the film at present admits only of naturalism in this respect.

d) *Colours and effects of light*

All the best works of Valle-Inclán conjure up extremely vivid mental pictures. The failure of a work like *La lámpara maravillosa* —notwithstanding its interest to the scholar— is explained by Valle's incapacity to express himself adequately in abstract terms. Granted that he saw with a painter's eye, it is understandable that he should have interested himself in effects of light and colour contrasts. This feature is already much in evidence in his *modernista* phase. It is an aspect of *Modernismo* which he never rejected, although he did modify his use of this and other stylistic features so as to establish a harmony between them and the tenets of his new aesthetic. Frequently, colours and light effects are charged with symbolism, and it is chiefly with these that I shall be concerned. One such has already been mentioned, namely, the *reductio ad absurdum* of the individual by referring to him as a *sombra.*

In the first chapter I drew a parallel between the imagery of Gabriel Miró and that of Valle-Inclán. In the works of both writers the images attached to particular characters indicate the author's veiled feelings towards them. I should now like to validate this point of contact by means of a specific example.

It has been pointed out that spectacles in Miró's novels indicate his dislike for the wearer: ". . . spectacles, . . . by their very nature tend to give the wearer a glazed look and form a barrier between him and the world."[47] Whilst Valle-Inclán does not use spectacles so consistently to indicate distaste on his part, there are examples of this symbolism in his works,[48] and of these the most interesting is to be found in *Tirano Banderas*: Niño Santos' eyes are never revealed for they are always hidden by dark spectacles. Visually, this increases his air of menace and his resemblance to a bird of fixed and vacant expression; morally, it suggests an abstraction, an impersonal, evil force rather than a human being. Significantly, the dark glasses are mentioned in the first description given of the Tyrant: "Inmóvil y taciturno . . . parece una calavera con antiparras negras y corbatín de

[47]Susan O'Sullivan, "Watches, Lemons and Spectacles: Recurrent Images in the Works of Gabriel Miró", *BHS*, XLIV (1967), 107-121.

[48]Valle applied an image of this kind to the satanic priest in the short story "Beatriz" (1903): "El canónigo sonrió levemente. La llama de las bujías brillaba en sus anteojos de oro" (I, 1255).

clérigo" (676). After this point there are very few allusions to his spectacles, although one of them emphasizes the inscrutable look which they give him: "La mirada, un misterio tras las verdosas anti-parras" (679). However, spectacles do not accompany him like the onomatopaeic 'chac, chac' as he chews his coca leaves, or terms such as *momia, cuáquero, lechuzo* and *calavera*. But having established the spectacles in the introductory description, this detail tends to remain in the reader's mind because it is well attuned to the other images applied to him.

It is also worth mentioning that two other unpleasant characters, both of them *gachupines,* wear spectacles. They are Quintín Pereda and the editor of the local Spanish newspaper, Don Nicolás Díaz del Rivero. Often, in Valle's works, the glint of light on metal hints at danger; thus the following description of Don Nicolás subtly indicates that he is on the side of evil: "Don Nicolás Díaz del Rivero pasaba el fulgor de sus quevedos sobre las cuartillas" (700).

A more obvious use of this kind of symbolism is the glint of light on a weapon, a stylistic device present even in Valle's earliest works. Here are two examples from *Tirano Banderas*:

> Prorrumpe en gritos, pero las luces de un puñal que ciega los ojos, la lengua le enfrenan (728).

> Al frente, sobre el flanco derecho, fulminaba el charrasco del Mayor Abilio del Valle (677).

Colours, like light, are used symbolically, and in all Valle's later works black and white assume the very greatest importance. On this subject Juan Guerrero Zamora writes: "Luz y sombra establecen no solo una jerarquía estética, sino también una diferenciación ética."[49] *Tirano Banderas* proves no exception in this respect owing to the emphasis on buzzards, bats, shadows, the murky recesses of Santa Mónica and, ever-present, the menacing bulk of the monastery: "A

---

[49]*Historia del teatro contemporáneo,* I, 190.

lo lejos . . . calcaba el negro perfil de su arquitectura San Martín de los
Mostenses"(819).

However, white does not necessarily connote virtue, for the Tyrant
is associated with this colour owing to certain words applied
metaphorically to him such as skull, parchment and wax. The
ambiguity of white is brought out in the following description where
Valle, like Miró, shows how the sun cannot penetrate the skin of a
man locked in the prison of self: "El Tirano, con el sol en la calavera,
fisgaba por los vidrios de la ventana" (790). White also assumes
unpleasant undertones when it is related to the coldness of the moon:
"El Tirano corría por el cielo el campo de su catalejo. Tenía blanca
de luna la calavera . . ." (713).

Another colour used consistently in this novel for its emblematic
value is green, but as with white it is applied in a rather ambiguous
fashion. Green normally denotes the erotic and to a large extent
this is what it conveys in *Tirano Banderas*. For example, in the
chapters centred on the depraved Spanish minister there are frequent
allusions to the legation's garden. The emblematic significance of
green emerges clearly in the following description of the garden,
haunted by the spirit of the lascivious vicereine: "Trepaban del
jardín verdes de una enredadera, y era detrás de los cristales toda la
sombra verde del jardín" (802).

The colour green has the same erotic connotations in the scenes
which take place in the bordello. Indeed the chapter devoted to it is
called 'La recámara verde', and it is in this green bedroom that Lupita
la Romántica and Nachito Veguillas make love. What appears, on
the surface, to confuse this straightforward use of green is the fact
that it is also associated with Santos Banderas: the seventh and last
section of the novel is entitled 'La mueca verde'. Faced with this
ambiguity, Vernon A. Chamberlin advances the following argument:
" . . . the green oozing from the corners of the dictator's mouth may
also have a deeper level of significance — an overflowing of deep-

seated, brutal and pernicious sensuality."[50] This may well be the correct explanation. Valle indicates the Tyrant's indifference or distaste for sexual matters through some of the images applied to him (*cuáquero, dómine*), and by his very real repugnance when he learns that Benicarlés is a homosexual and a transvestite: "Tirano Banderas, recogido en un gesto cuáquero, fulminó su excomunión:—¡ Aberraciones repugnantes! "(707). If the Tyrant has deliberately suppressed his sexuality, then, arguing along Freudian lines, this would account for the sadistic tendencies he manifests when, for instance, he watches an Indian being tortured, revels in the humiliation of Nachito or stabs his daughter fifteen times.

However, in a few cases, light effects and colour contrasts have a solely artistic purpose:

> Los cocuyos encendían su danza de luces en la borrosa y lunaria geometría del jardín (713).

> Y puesto el papel en el cono luminoso de la linterna, aplicó los ojos el patrón (671).

> Las niñas del pecado, desmadejadas y desdeñosas, recogían el bulle-bulle en el vaivén de las mecedoras: el rojo de los cigarros las señalaba en sus lugares (717).

> Un vaho pesado . . . anunciaba la proximidad de la manigua, donde el crepúsculo enciende, con las estrellas, los ojos de los jaguares (690).

[50]"Symbolic Green: a time-honored characterizing device in Spanish literature", *Hispania* (U.S.A.), LI (1968), 29-37.

IX

Linguistic Features

a) *Towards a Hispanic language*

The language used in *Tirano Banderas* might be described as elegant and well-assembled pastiche. Since Valle was so acutely sensitive to the musical value of words, it must have given him considerable satisfaction vastly to increase the resources of Castilian Spanish by incorporating terms from all over Spanish America. Emma Speratti has pointed out that the concept of *americanismos* in this novel is acceptable only in its widest sense: " . . . admite, dentro del funcionamiento del habla americana, arcaísmos, neologismos, localismos peninsulares y voces extranjeras, siempre que el arraigo de su empleo lo justifique."[51]

This forging of a Hispanic tongue allows the author to make all sorts of subtle points and to create strange effects which would have been unattainable had he limited himself to peninsular Spanish. One obvious example of the benefits derived from these accretions to the language is the effective use Valle makes of diminutives such as 'generalito', 'Peredita' and 'Gandarita'. These are permissible owing to the Mexicans' fondness for this particular suffix.

A further advantage stemming from these additions is that the language employed by characters in a fit of anger strikes the reader as more forceful owing to its freshness and to the strange amalgam of words and verbal forms from different parts of the sub-continent. This point is particularly relevant in the case of Niño Santos. The coarseness of the Tyrant's expressions in these violent outbursts forms a marked contrast with the very formal and ornate speech he usually adopts. They are among the few glimpses allowed the reader

[51]*La elaboración artística en Tirano Banderas,* 107.

of the brutal, unbalanced man behind the "máscara indiana". I shall quote some examples of the Tyrant's abusive language when enraged, contrasting these with the language he uses when his spirit is serene:

Reprimanding a servant:

> ¡Chingada, guarda tenés de la niña! ¡Hi de tal, la tenés bien guardada! (713)

and addressing a group of *gachupines*:

> —Me congratula ver como los hermanos de raza aquí radicados, afirmando su fe inquebrantable en los ideales de orden y progreso, responden a la tradición de la Madre Patria (678).

Showering abuse on his soldiers:

> — ¡A las estrellas tiráis, hijos de la chingada! (829)

and seeking to ingratiate himself with Don Roque:

> —Mi señor Don Roque, recién me entero de su detención en el fuerte. ¡Lo he deplorado! Hágame el honor de considerarme ajeno a esa molestia. Santos Banderas guarda todos los miramientos a un repúblico tan ameritado, y nuestras diferencias ideológicas no son tan irreductibles como usted parece presuponerlo, mi señor Don Roque (793).

The variety of *americanismos* also serves to add a very exotic touch to some of the descriptive passages in the book. The window of Quintín Pereda's shop is "luciente de arracadas, *fistoles* y *mancuernas,* guarnecido de pistolas y puñales, colgado de *ñandutis* y *zarapes*",[52] and in a country of cacti, jaguars and tropical swamps, the llama makes an unexpected appearance: "Por los crepusculares caminos de tierra roja ondulaban recuas de llamas, piños vacunos, tropas de jinetes con el sol poniente en los sombreros bordados de plata" (763).

b) *The parody of debased language and literature*

When Valle-Inclán was in his late fifties and startling the Spanish literary scene by producing his most original, dynamic and memorable

---

[52]Fistol: tie-pin (Mexico); mancuernas: cuff-links (Mexico and Central America); ñanduti: very fine lace-work (Paraguay and River Plate); zarape: brightly coloured poncho or rug (Mexico and Guatemala).

works, he developed an almost passionate dislike of bad nineteenth-century fiction and drama (the younger Dumas, Sue, Echegaray, Zorrilla) and of grandiloquent poetry (Espronceda and Darío). This dislike of the content is reflected in parodies of the styles of these and other writers, which frequently take the form of using quotations from their works, like a painter applying *collages* to a canvas. Since the art of writing was to him almost a religious cult, it is understandable that he should have parodied the styles not only of what were, in his view, bad writers, but, in addition, the jargon used by politicians and journalists. In these cases he felt that language was being reduced to a series of meaningless, ritualistic platitudes which the mind refused to absorb because they were stale and unimaginatively handled. There are examples of all these forms of linguistic parody in *Tirano Banderas.*

The writers and poets who come under fire in this novel are first and foremost Espronceda and, to a lesser extent, Rubén Darío and Alexandre Dumas. The last of these is only referred to in passing, more prominence being given to him in the *Ruedo ibérico* cycle. In *Tirano Banderas* Dumas is mentioned when Niño Santos refuses to swallow Nachito's account of how Lupita la Romántica read his thoughts. At this point the Tyrant exclaims ironically " ¡Estamos en un folletín de Alejandro Dumas! " (820). However, just as in the *esperpento* of *Las galas del difunto* Valle devotes most of his attention to parodying Zorrilla's *Don Juan Tenorio,* so here it is the poetry of Espronceda which is ridiculed most frequently. The 'Canción del pirata' with its message of swashbuckling revolt and total liberty is parodied in the novel's prologue by being put in the mouth of a lisping negro:

> Navega veleĺo mío
>   sin temol
> que ni enemigo navío
> ni tolmenta, ni bonanza,
> a tolcel tu lumbo alcanza
> ni a sujetal tu valol (675).

Espronceda's poetry is ridiculed once again in 'La recámara verde'
when Nachito, in bed with Lupita, quotes from *El estudiante de
Salamanca,* exclaiming "Angel puro de amor que amor inspira" (724).
Lines from Espronceda's poetry are also recalled, although imperfectly
quoted to accentuate the satire, when Nachito describes Lupita as an
"ángel que tienes rotas las alas". This is based on a stanza from the
'Canto a Teresa' in which Espronceda compares Teresa to a fallen
angel: "es la mujer ángel caído". Espronceda's poem about a
prostitute, 'A Jarifa en una orgía', finds an echo in the same scene
when Nachito, by this time quite maudlin, says:

> ¡Bésame Jarifa! ¡Bésame, impúdica, inocente! ¡Dame un ósculo
> casto y virginal! ¡Caminaba solo por el desierto de la vida, y se me
> aparece un oasis de amor, donde reposar la frente!

At this juncture the author makes a tart comment through the mouth
of Lupita:

> Nachito sollozaba, y la del trato, para consolarle, le dio un beso de
> folletín romántico, apretándole a la boca el corazón de su boca
> pintado. ¡Eres sonso! (725).

With great subtlety Valle introduces another kind of mawkish
sentimentality and its neutraliser into the background of this chapter.
For acting as point and counterpoint are the song of Velones'
daughter:

> ¡No me mates, traidora ilusión!
> Es tu imagen en mi pensamiento
> una hoguera de casta pasión;

and the grim ballad about the crime of Diego Pedernales:

> En borrico de justicia
> le sacan con un pregón
> hizo mamola al verdugo
> al revestirle el jopón
> y al Cristo que le presentaban,
> una seña de masón (719).

This ballad, from which I have quoted only the last stanza, recalls
a poem in *La pipa de kif* (1919) entitled 'El crimen de Medinica'.
The ballad in *Tirano Banderas* is in keeping with the *esperpento*'s

vision of humanity, whilst the other song is a symbol of the false
emotions which Valle attacks as much in 'La recámara verde' as
elsewhere in his later works.

It is not unusual for Valle to quote from Darío's poetry or to be
influenced by it. He even introduces Rubén as a character in his play
Luces de bohemia (1920). However, as Valle had been a great
admirer of Darío, it is unusual for him to refer to his poetry and the
sentiments expressed in it in a sardonic manner, this being what
occurs in *Tirano Banderas*. There is an allusion to Darío's poem
'Salutación al águila' in the scene which takes place in the British
Legation. At one point the handsome Ecuadorian Minister, Doctor
Aníbal Roncali, suggests that the representatives of the various Latin-
American states should have a meeting of their own. He describes
their group as "Las águilas jóvenes que tendían las alas para el
heróico vuelo, agrupadas en torno del águila materna" (807). These
lines are based on Darío's

> Bien vengas, mágica Aguila de las alas enormes y fuertes,
> a extender sobre el Sur tu gran sombra continental . . .
> Que la latina América reciba tu mágica influencia
> y que renazca nuevo Olimpo, lleno de dioses y héroes.

At a later point Aníbal Roncali tells Carlos Esparza, the Uruguayan
Minister, about his embarrassment over Benicarlés' sexual advances.
He adds that for this reason he is reluctant to accept the post of
secretary on the committee which will have the Baron as its chair-
man. Esparza proceeds to pull Roncali's leg, referring sardonically to
the latter's speech that afternoon:

> Repito que no te asiste razón suficiente para malograr una aproxi-
> mación de tan lindas esperanzas. El águila y los aguiluchos que
> abren las juveniles alas para el heroico vuelo. ¡Has estado muy
> feliz! ¡Eres un gran lírico! (816).

Esparza then emphasizes his point by adding:

> ¡Lírico, sentimental, sensitivo, sensible! —exclamaba el Cisne de
> Nicaragua—. Por eso, no logras vos separar la actuación diplomática
> y el flirt del Ministro de España (816).

'Sentimental, sensible, sensitiva' is a line from Darío's poem 'Yo soy aquel que ayer no más decía', the first poem in the collection *Cantos de vida y esperanza* (1905).

I mentioned in an earlier chapter that satire of politicians' jargon is centred on Sánchez Ocaña. The most amusing example of his empty rhetoric is to be found in a scene in which he addresses his fellow-prisoners in Santa Mónica. This passage is worth quoting at some length:

> —El funesto fénix del absolutismo colonial renace de sus cenizas aventadas a los cuatro vientos, concitando las sombras y los manes de los augustos libertadores. Augustos, sí, y el ejemplo de sus vidas debe servirnos de luminar en estas horas, que acaso son las últimas que nos resta vivir. El mar devuelve a la tierra sus héroes, los voraces monstruos de las azules minas se muestran más piadosos que el general Santos Banderas ... Nuestros ojos ...
> Se interrumpía. Llegaba por el corredor la pata de palo. El Alcalde cruzó fumando en cachimba, y poco a poco extinguióse el alerta de su paso cojitranco (777).

Here Valle uses the same technique of abrupt anti-climax as when Lupita, after enduring Nachito's drunken eloquence, remarks crisply " ¡Eres sonso!"

Whilst pedantic speech is satirised mainly through the language employed by Niño Santos, a further example is afforded by the insistence of Don Nicolás, the newspaper editor, on maintaining the purity of the Spanish language. When a junior reporter on his staff shows him his account of the political meeting at the Harris Circus, Don Nicolás reprimands him both for a certain note of sincerity and also for his careless style. Once more, in order to retain the flavour of the passage, it is best to quote from it at some length:

> Le falta a usted intención política. Nosotros no podemos decir que el público premió con una ovación la presencia del Licenciado Sánchez Ocaña. Puede usted escribir: Los aplausos oficiosos de algunos amigos no lograron ocultar el fracaso de tan difusa pieza oratoria, que tuvo de todo menos de ciceroniana. Es una redacción de elemental formulario. ¡Cada día es usted menos periodista!
> El Vate Larrañaga sonrió tímidamente:

— ¡Y temía haberme excedido en la censura!
El Director repasaba las cuartillas.
—Tuvo lugar es un galicismo.
Rectificó complaciente el Vate:
—Tuvo verificativo.
—No lo admite la Academia (700).

Literature has been defined as a critical response to language, and this definition neatly summarises at least one important objective of Valle-Inclán's in *Tirano Banderas*. Before serious attention was paid to his later works it was fashionable to dismiss Valle as primarily, if not entirely, a stylist. In a novel like *Tirano Banderas* the sensitivity to language remains in the forefront, but it is enhanced by the subject matter which, unlike that of the *Sonatas,* could not be dismissed by the author as mere "musiquilla de violín".

X

Conclusion

Despite the grimness of its theme, little sympathy is felt for the characters in *Tirano Banderas*. The fact that the reader's emotions are in no way engaged does not, however, indicate a failure of communication on the part of Valle-Inclán. He chose, quite deliberately, to alienate the reader in the Brechtian sense by raising an artistic barrier between him and the material. This successfully prevents identification with the characters.

In this, as in all Valle's mature works, two features stand out at all times: the extraordinary artistry and polish of the novel; secondly, its devastating satire. The artistry is reflected above all in the author's ability to create the most vivid verbal pictures. The importance of the plastic element in Valle's works causes Francisco Umbral to form the following very shrewd conclusions:

> Su mente y su retina se cargan de imágenes con una riqueza y diversidad asombrosas ... Su gran inteligencia es una inteligencia plástica que puede llegar muy lejos por este camino, pero que vacila y se pierde en las raras ocasiones en que quiere desnudarse de formas y actuar como inteligencia pura. Así la frase de André Gide, "mi ética es mi estética" se hará verdad en Valle como en nadie.[53]

La lámpara maravillosa (1916), a volume Valle devoted to his aesthetic, is one of the few books in which he sought to express himself in abstract terms. As Umbral implies, whilst of interest to students of his work, it is also muddled and tedious. In my opinion, it is precisely because the character of Roque Cepeda is an embodiment of the preoccupations expressed in *La lámpara maravillosa,* that he is among the less convincing characters in *Tirano Banderas*. There is a vague, nebulous quality about him which contrasts with the vividness

---

[53] *Valle-Inclán* (Madrid, 1968), 32.

of the other major characters.

Umbral and other critics consider that Valle's satire has an ethical basis. On the other hand, Antonio Risco argues that Valle's vision is totally nihilistic. All that emerges from his later works is a blanket condemnation of Spain or, in his own words, a "condena de la barbarie ibérica".[54] In this respect Risco thinks that Valle differs from Quevedo: the latter is a moralist, whilst Valle-Inclán is basically amoral. Valle's satire is destructive; he puts forward no solutions save for the rather unsatisfactory one of finding refuge and solace in art.

In the case of *Tirano Banderas* it is frankly unjust to term Valle nihilistic and destructive. Certainly he is deeply pessimistic, certainly he pours scorn on most of his characters, certainly scenes of chaos like the riot at the Harris Circus and the description of the rebels entering Santa Fe reflect his view of the world as chaos. But one must also take into account the following points: Valle's sympathy for the downtrodden Indians is palpably sincere, and those attempting to improve their lot do not suffer the degradation of 'esperpentización'. It would seem that when Valle reflected on Spain in the nineteen-twenties he registered only deep despair; when he turned his attention to the New World he appeared to retain at least some measure of enthusiasm and hope.

[54]*La estética de Valle-Inclán*, 21.

Bibliographical Note

a) *General*

Diáz-Plaja, Guillermo. *Las estéticas de Valle-Inclán* (Madrid, 1965). Studies the evolution of Valle's works as reflected in his changing attitude towards his central characters.

Fernández Almagro, Melchor. *Vida y literatura de Valle-Inclán* (Madrid, 1943). Reprinted in 1966. Straightforward and quite reliable work by a contemporary of the author.

Umbral, Francisco. *Valle-Inclán* (Madrid, 1968). A brief and unpretentious introduction to the writer and his works. Shows considerable insight at times when considering the essentials of Valle's art.

Zahareas, Anthony (ed.). *Ramón del Valle-Inclán* (New York, 1968). A very comprehensive survey of Valle-Inclán's works. It includes a number of articles, some of high quality, which refer either directly or indirectly to *Tirano Banderas*.

b) *Detailed Studies*

Balseiro, José. *Cuatro individualistas de España* (Chapel Hill, 1949). The essay on Valle-Inclán contains comments on *Tirano Banderas* with particular reference to Cubism and the use of cinematographic techniques.

Chamberlin, Vernon A. "Symbolic Green: a time-honored characterizing device in Spanish Literature", *Hispania* (U.S.A.), LI (1968), 29-37. Considers symbolic use of this colour in *Tirano Banderas*.

Falconieri, John V. "*Tirano Banderas*: su estructura esperpéntica", *Quaderni Ibero-Americani,* IV (1962), 203-207. Argues that time stands still throughout the novel.

Franco, Jean. "The Concept of Time in *El ruedo ibérico*", *Bulletin of Hispanic Studies,* XXXIX (1962), 177-87. Concerned with Valle-Inclán's application of number symbolism to the structure of the two completed novels of this unfinished cycle.

Guerrero Zamora, Juan. *Historia del teatro contemporáneo,* I (Barcelona, 1961), 153-206. A stimulating analysis of the genesis of the *esperpento*, its significance and the techniques Valle-Inclán adopted to express his viewpoint.

Gullón, Ricardo. "Técnicas de Valle-Inclán", *Papeles de Son Armadans,* XLIII (1966), 21-86. A penetrating analysis of *Tirano Banderas* in which Gullón is concerned with four levels of understanding: the narrative, the historic, the fantastic and the symbolic.

Lagmanovich, David. "La visión de América en *Tirano Banderas*", *Humanitas* (Tucumán, Argentina), III (1955), 267-278. Interesting comments on the significance of the novel's highly stylised background.

March, María Eugenia. *Forma e idea de los esperpentos de Valle-Inclán* (Valencia, 1969). The introductory chapters, concerned with the development of the *esperpento* vision, are relevant to *Tirano Banderas.*

Marías, Julian. *Valle-Inclán en el ruedo ibérico* (Buenos Aires, 1967). A brief, illuminating and very readable analysis of Valle's aims and techniques in the historical novels of his maturity.

Risco, Antonio. *La estética de Valle-Inclán* (Madrid, 1966). Particularly interesting on the significance of certain grammatical features of Valle-Inclán's later novels.

Salinas, Pedro. "Significación del *esperpento* o Valle-Inclán hijo pródigo del '98", *Literatura española siglo XX* (México, 1949), 87-114. A general survey of the *esperpento,* the spirit which informs it and the connotations of the style Valle adopted in his maturity.

Speratti Piñero, Emma Susana. *La elaboración artística en Tirano Banderas* (México, 1957). Reprinted in *De "Sonata de otoño" al esperpento (Aspectos del arte de Valle-Inclán)* (London, Colección Támesis, 1968). To date the only volume devoted exclusively to this novel. Indispensable reading for those interested in *Tirano Banderas.*